A CLOUD OF WITNESSES

A CLOUD OF WITNESSES

Ten Great Christian Thinkers

ALISTER E. McGRATH

ZondervanPublishingHouse

Academic and Professional Books

Grand Rapids, Michigan

A Division of HarperCollinsPublishers

A Cloud of Witnesses
Copyright © 1990 by Alister E. McGrath
Originally published in England by Inter-Varsity Press

Requests for information should be addressed to:
Zondervan Publishing House
Academic and Professional Books
1415 Lake Drive S.E.
Grand Rapids, Michigan 49506

Library of Congress Cataloging-in-Publication Data

McGrath Alister E., 1953-
    A cloud of witnesses : ten great Christian thinkers / Alister
McGrath.
      p.   cm.
    Includes bibliographical references.
    ISBN 0-310-29671-4
    1. Theology, Doctrinal–Popular works.   2. Theologians.
I. Title.
BT77.M38   1990
230–dc20
                                      90-45346
                                        CIP

Printed in the United States of America

90 91 92 93 94 95 / PP / 10 9 8 7 6 5 4 3 2 1

Contents

Introduction

FOR many Christians, history and theology are both something of an irrelevance. To deepen your understanding of our faith, they suggest, all that you need do is read the Bible. There is no need to study history or theology. The present has enough problems without worrying about the past! So what is the point in looking at great Christian thinkers of the past?

It must be admitted that there is a lot to be said for this viewpoint. One of the best ways of deepening your faith is by reading the Bible. Writer after writer has commented on how you can read the same scriptural book time after time, without it becoming stale or uninteresting. Each time round, you notice something new. Something strikes you which you hadn't noticed before. Not all literature is like that!

I remember once living in a country house in the outskirts of Utrecht, in the Netherlands, for about five weeks. I didn't speak Dutch (and, to my shame, I still don't), and so was delighted when I found a handful of English novels to read in my spare time. And because there was nothing else available for me to read, I had to read them again and again – and I must admit that I found they got rather tedious the third time round! But with Scripture, what happens seems to be rather different. You get used to the text. And as the words and images it uses become more and more familiar to you, you begin to notice more. You become aware of its depth, of its various levels of meaning. It's like looking at an Old Master – once you get used to the main features of the painting, you begin to notice more of its fine detail. You appreciate it more. You can discern things which had previously passed unnoticed.

So why bother with other writers? Scripture, you may say, is perfectly adequate on its own. (If you are more theologically-minded already, you might argue that Scripture was materially sufficient in itself.) Perhaps it might help to imagine the following situation. You are in a Bible study, with a group of people. You are all studying the same passage. And someone points out something that you hadn't noticed before. New light is suddenly shed on familiar material. Perhaps someone else might then come up with a way of looking at a passage which hadn't occured to you. And you realize that, left to yourself, you'd have missed that. That is why the riches of Scripture are best uncovered in company, with each person present stimulating others and learning from them.

One person might tell the group how a certain problem has always been a particular difficulty; someone else in the group might then be able to explain that problem, or give a really helpful way of looking at it. Can you imagine how useful that can be? Most of us have had some sort of experience like that. Other people help us understand both Scripture and our faith more deeply. It helps to study Scripture and think about the gospel in good company – and this book aims to put you in good company as you think through some key areas of the Christian faith.

Reading about the great Christian thinkers of the past is like being at a really good Bible study. They can help you think through things you may have been puzzled by. They can cast new light on a familiar scriptural passage. They can inspire us with their testimonies – for some of the people we'll be looking at have very fine stories to tell about how they became Christians. They can stretch your thinking, helping you wrestle with important questions which you ought to think through at some point. What better way to begin, than to be introduced to a classic discussion of such questions?

Every now and then, most of us find ourselves turning to a biblical commentary to make sense of a biblical passage, or to work out how it relates to another which seems to state something slightly different. Karl Barth, one of the writers to be studied in this work, suggests that we think of systematic theology as an extended commentary on Scripture. The doctrine of the Trinity, for example, brings together the richness of the scriptural passages dealing with God, and shows how they relate to one another. Theology, in other words, attempts to weave the threads of Scripture into a single garment. It tries to bring together the biblical statements on subjects of major importance, and demonstrate how they make up a consistent whole.

An interest in theology, then, in no way threatens your natural interest in studying Scripture. In fact, it offers you the chance to deepen your knowledge and understanding of Scripture, by helping you to think through how various biblical passages relate to one another. It is not realistic to expect to be able to summarize the entire Christian teaching on any subject by quoting a single biblical reference. What single biblical reference, for example, could you choose to sum up the scriptural teaching on the meaning and relevance of the death of Jesus Christ? To do justice to the richness of this subject, a whole range of biblical material would have to be marshalled together. Theology is an attempt to gather together all the relevant material, and make sense of it.

Theology integrates Scripture. In other words, it brings together the kaleidoscope of scriptural statements on any subject, and allows us to see their common pattern. It identifies the great unifying themes underlying biblical passages, and shows how any particular passage illustrates such a theme. To be a theologian is not to dispense with Scripture, but to become so immersed in it that its common themes and patterns begin to emerge.

All of us try to think about our faith at times. Perhaps you have tried to explain your faith to someone else, and found yourself wishing that you really understood it better yourself. It is much easier to explain something when you have thought it through yourself! Or you may be trying to understand some aspect of your faith – for example, what the best way of explaining the meaning of the death and resurrection of Jesus Christ might be. And as you do this, you have probably found yourself thinking along these lines: surely I'm not the first person ever to try and think this one through! There must have been other people who've wrestled with these questions. And you may have found yourself wondering what answers they gave, in case they're of any use today.

Your suspicion is certainly well grounded. There are actually relatively few *new* questions facing Christians. Most of the relevant questions that Christians face today confronted Christians in the past as well. And some of the answers given in the past are helpful today. This book aims to introduce you to some classic replies to some of those questions – replies which will be helpful in stimulating your own thinking. You can think through some central areas of the Christian faith in good company, letting the ideas of people such as John Calvin or C. S. Lewis stimulate and inform your own thinking. Their ideas can serve as markers, as points of reference, for your own thinking. They can also lend more weight to your own thoughts. It adds credibility to your case if you can quote an established authority in its support. To be able to say, 'C. S. Lewis makes the point that ...', or 'Martin Luther says that ...', is much more impressive than saying, '*I* think that ...'!

Sometimes you will find memorable quotes that may cast new light on a subject, or sum up a point particularly neatly. Sometimes you will encounter an argument you hadn't thought of before, which may get you really excited. Please don't keep them to yourself. This book aims to make available some important Christian resources, which are of continuing use within the Christian church today. If something you read about in this book is helpful, pass it on to your friends.

The New Testament frequently emphasizes our need to grow in faith. Just as an infant feeds on milk until it is weaned (1 Cor. 3:2; Heb. 5:12; 1 Pet. 2:2), so young Christians need to absorb some very simple ideas about their faith. As they grow, however, they need to move on. Just as weaned infants begin to be able to (and *need* to) cope with solid food if they are to grow, so you need to progress from very simple ideas about Christianity. 'Let us leave the elementary teachings about Christ and go on to maturity' (Heb. 6:1). Not everyone needs to go deeper into their faith; not everyone is able to. Some lack the time, others the intellectual ability, to think deeply about their faith. But if

God has given you the time and the ability to do so, you could become an important resource person for your church or Christian community – because you have thought through some key issues which are relevant to preaching the gospel, thinking about God, and living out a Christian life in the world.

It should also be stressed that theology without faith is dead and irrelevant. Augustine of Hippo once wrote 'unless you believe, you shall never understand'. True theology presupposes faith. One of the greatest weaknesses of some academic theology is its failure to relate to Christian life and experience. As a result, it loses its vital link with the realities of Christian existence. One of the reasons why many Christians distrust theology is that they rightly sense that some of its practicioners have little interest in the gospel. That is a perfectly valid criticism of those theologians, but not of theology itself.

Anselm of Canterbury, writing in the eleventh century, suggested that faith seeks understanding. Once an individual comes to faith, there is a natural desire to understand what has been believed. Faith is indeed caught, rather than taught; but once caught, it must be allowed to develop. Faith needs intellectual muscle and stamina if it is to grow and mature. Faith is like reinforced concrete. Concrete which is reinforced with a steel framework is able to stand far greater stress and strain than concrete on its own. Faith which is reinforced with understanding will not crumble easily under pressure. Again, faith is like the flesh and bones of a human body. Just as the human skeleton supports the flesh, giving it shape and strength, so understanding supports and gives shape to the Christian experience. Beginning to study theology is like body-building exercises, or training for a long-distance run: it gets you in shape to meet the needs of the Christian life.

Every book is written with a definite readership in mind. This is not a book for theologians, who will probably already be familiar with everything in its pages and have read most of the suggestions for further reading. It lacks the sophistication and depth necessary for college and university examinations. It isn't meant to be read by people with such needs. Rather, it is a book for *potential* theologians, for people who want to deepen their understanding of their faith and begin to think through some key areas of Christian thought. It is hoped that the simplicity and lightness of touch of the present work will help you realize that you *can* cope with theological ideas and arguments. It is meant to whet your appetite on the one hand, and disarm your fears about theology on the other. Despite everything you may have been told, theology can be *fun*, it can be *relevant* to your faith, and it can be *helpful* in the task of building up individuals and communities in their faith.

But where do you start? And who should you read? Theology, after all, includes some material that is tedious, virtually unreadable, muddled, irresponsible or simply absurd. You need guidance as to where to start. As a university teacher of theology, I am only too painfully aware of the dangers of people being put off the subject permanently through beginning with an unsuitable writer. Early impressions are important in shaping later attitudes. In order to stimulate you to want to read more, the writers included in this work have been selected on the basis of the interest they generate in students at Oxford.

In this book, you will find some of the ideas of ten leading Christian thinkers presented, along with information about their lives and times which will help bring them alive as individuals. (Sometimes, however, as with Athanasius and Anselm of Canterbury, the writers chosen are of importance mainly on account of their ideas, so that these chapters are relatively weak on biographical material.) Although they are all dead, they can still speak to us. They are a 'cloud of witnesses' (Heb. 12:1) to the Christian faith. Some of them are perhaps not as reliable witnesses as others, but you can rest assured that they are all interesting and important, and likely to help you grow in intellectual maturity as a Christian. Their witness to the gospel can help *your* witness to that same gospel, just as their ideas and approaches may help you develop your own understanding of your faith.

The chapters are all designed to be capable of being read at a single session, and assume you know little, if anything, about either the thinker or his ideas. This book aims to introduce the men and their ideas, in the belief that you will find at least some of them – and quite possibly all of them – helpful to your thinking. It allows you to sample their ideas. Each of the thinkers casts light on different areas of the Christian faith. Some will stimulate your thinking about grace and sin; others will help you think through the meaning of the death of Christ; others will illuminate the relation of faith and reason.

You will notice that each chapter ends with suggestions for further reading. In every case, you will be told where to find out more about the thinker and his ideas. In most cases, you will also be told what books by the more recent thinkers currently available will help you understand more about him, or stimulate your thinking about the issue being raised. Many of these writers – especially the more recent ones – are very prolific, and it helps to be told where to start!

Finally, remember that this book aims only to get you started. It is meant to serve as a taster, to stimulate your appetite to think and learn more. It will unlock a door, and give a foretaste of what lies beyond. It will have served its purpose if you want to take things further, by passing through that door to investigate what lies beyond with the care and attention it deserves. A final section thus gives guidance on how to proceed from here, to discover the riches and rewards that theology can offer to responsible individuals and communities. For if theology is indeed 'talk about God' (as its Greek root suggests), there can be few more rewarding and relevant undertakings awaiting the Christian.

Alister McGrath
Oxford

CHAPTER ONE

ATHANASIUS:

The Divinity of Christ

CHRISTIANITY exploded into the Mediterranean world in the first century. No other word does justice to the way in which the Christian faith spread so rapidly throughout the civilized world of the period. Even within the New Testament, the beginnings of this enormous expansion may be traced. The first Christians saw their task as bringing 'salvation to the ends of the earth' (Acts 13:47), and even during the period of the New Testament itself, the gospel was achieving remarkable successes.

From its origins in Palestine, the gospel rapidly spread through the efforts of the first Christians. The seven churches referred to in the book of Revelation (Rev. 1:10–11; 2:1 – 3:22) are all located in that part of the world which is modern-day Turkey. Paul's letters to the Galatians and Ephesians were also addressed to communities in the same area; his letters to the Corinthians, Philippians and Thessalonians were all addressed to Christian communities in the area covered by modern-day Greece. His letter to the Roman Christian community demonstrates how Christianity found its way to the heart of the Roman empire within a remarkably short period after the resurrection. Paul's missionary journeys contributed to this rapid expansion – Paul even wrote of his plans to travel as far west as Spain (Rom. 15:24) to proclaim the gospel at this western extremity of the Mediterranean.

Others, however, were proclaiming the gospel as well as Paul. When Paul wrote to the Roman Christians sometime around the year 58, he was writing to a church which he himself hadn't planted. It was already there. We don't know exactly how the gospel got to Rome. Some say that Peter arrived there in the year 42. By the year 64, the Christians were such a large section of the community that their presence could not be ignored by the Roman authorities. A general persecution of Christians got under way in the city under Nero in the year 64. It is thought that both Peter and Paul were martyred in Rome by Nero around this time.

Christianity had to fight for its life at many points during its expansion in these early years, as it encountered considerable hostility. Many leading figures of the church were martyred on account of their faith. Tertullian, a leading third century Christian writer based in the African city of Carthage, wrote that 'the blood of the martyrs is the seed of the church'. In other words, martyrs draw attention to the claims of the gospel, and the impact it makes upon people's lives. The early Christians showed enormous courage in the face of death, reflecting their faith in the resurrection of Jesus Christ. And people noticed. Their witness made a profound impression at the time, making no small contribution to the spread of the Christian faith.

Christianity was not spread at the point of the sword – in fact, the sword was used almost entirely *against* Christians in the first centuries, as various Roman emperors and governors tried to suppress the Christian faith. It owed its survival and spread to the power of the gospel itself. There was something enormously attractive about the Christian gospel, especially its proclamation of the resurrection of Jesus. Somehow, it seemed to resonate with the hopes and fears of the peoples of the Mediterranean world and beyond. The appeal of this inherent attractiveness of the gospel was complemented by the lifestyle of believers. Perseverance in the face of persecution resulted in Christian influence becoming considerable throughout the Mediterranean by the third century.

At the beginning of the fourth century, the influence of Christianity became of decisive importance to the Roman

Empire. One event which both reflected and contributed to this growing influence was the conversion of Constantine, who would eventually become emperor. Just before a vicious battle against invading barbarians, probably in France in the year 311, Constantine had a vision. As he prepared for the conflict, he saw a cross outlined against the face of the midday sun, with the words 'By this conquer' inscribed upon it. By the spring of the following year, Constantine was openly proclaiming his conversion to the gospel. Upon his triumphant entry into Rome in October of that year to claim the imperial throne, he had a statue of himself erected in a public square, a cross in his hand. Where the emperors had once fought to eliminate the gospel, they now showed an equal determination to establish it. With the conversion of Constantine, Christianity gained the status of the official religion of the Roman Empire.

It is very difficult for the ordinary Christian not to see the hand of God at work in the way Christianity expanded. Paul speaks of Jesus Christ coming in the 'fulness of time' or 'when the times will have reached their fulfilment' (Eph. 1:10) – in other words, when the time was right. The world of the first half of the first century was ideally suited to the rapid spread of the good news about Jesus Christ. It was a relatively peaceful period; there were excellent trade routes available; there was a common language (Greek) by which news could be spread. The success of Paul's three missionary journeys illustrates these three points very well.

'*Greek*? Isn't that a very *difficult* language?', many people ask. Not if it's the language you learned from birth! It just looks difficult to outsiders, not least on account of its unfamiliar alphabet. English is widely regarded as one of the most difficult modern languages, a fact which most English speakers find hard to understand. One of the reasons why so many people learn English as their second language is that it is of vital importance for trade, diplomacy and culture – just as Greek was in the first century world. The New Testament was written in a language which most of the civilized world could understand.

Christianity, then, moved northwards and westwards

from its origins in Jerusalem, becoming established in the areas covered by modern-day Turkey, Greece and Italy. It also moved south. One of the countries in which Christianity became firmly planted as a result of this expansion was Egypt – and it was here that a major controversy developed during the fourth century, just as Constantine established Christianity as the religion of the Roman Empire. This controversy centred upon two figures: Athanasius and his opponent Arius. It has passed into history as the Arian controversy. The central question at stake was whether Jesus really was divine. Was Jesus just a splendid man, or was he God incarnate? What difference does it make, anyway? Such questions have a habit of reappearing throughout history, making this particular controversy of especial importance. In this chapter, we're going to look at some of the main points debated, and their importance today.

One of the major questions puzzling many people in the intellectual world of the first few centuries centred on how anybody could know anything about God. Platonism – one of the most important movements of the time – generally taught that God was remote and unknowable. He couldn't reveal himself. He was distant. He was transcendent – in other words, totally apart from this world. So how could anybody know anything about him?

One of the reasons that Christianity was so attractive at the time was that it could give a straight answer to this question. God has revealed himself. He has spoken to us. The letter to the Hebrews is sometimes thought to have the interests and worries of Platonists at heart. On reading the first few verses (Heb. 1:1–4), it is easy to see why Christianity was so exciting for such people. God had revealed himself in Jesus Christ. Jesus is the 'exact representation of his being'. In other words, if you want to find out what God is like, look at Jesus. And maybe Paul has the same Platonic problem in mind with his famous words, spoken at Athens: 'what you worship as something unknown, I am going to proclaim to you' (Acts 17:23).

Perhaps it is difficult at first to see why this should have been thought of as so important and exciting. Human

17

beings have found it remarkably difficult to think about God. The philosophers of the ancient world debated endlessly (as their modern equivalents still do) as to what God was like. As God could not be seen or heard, it was rather difficult to think seriously about him. When Christianity arrived on the scene, it brought with it the news that God had taken the initiative. Instead of human beings having to search for God, the gospel declared that he had come searching for humanity. He had made himself known to all who were prepared to discover him in Jesus Christ. As the 'image of the invisible God' (Col. 1:15), Jesus was able to make known what had hitherto been unknown, or at best known in a partial and fragmentary manner.

In order for Jesus to inform us what God is like, he must have some special sort of relationship with God. There must be something about him that sets him apart, that makes him and his ideas about God carry authority and weight. He is not like some sort of newspaper article, telling us about God at second hand. The New Testament declares that in Jesus the 'Word became flesh' (Jn. 1:14) – in other words, God became incarnate. Jesus tells us about God, and shows us what God is like, precisely because he *is* God. He doesn't need to tell us about God at second hand, in the manner of an envoy or delegate. By the beginning of the fourth century, the doctrine of the incarnation had become widely accepted as the best way of understanding who Jesus was, and why he was so important. Here was none other than God himself, in human form.

But was this right? Was Jesus really divine? Was he really God incarnate? Some had their doubts, and began to raise questions. A debate developed in the fourth century over this question, with Arius leading those who felt the idea of incarnation was unnecessary. Arius' personal popularity lent support to his case: he had a considerable following among Egyptian dockers (for whom he wrote sea-shanties with religious themes) and young women. Arius was convinced that the New Testament regarded Jesus as a particularly splendid human being. He wasn't God incarnate, or anything like that. He was one of God's creatures, just like us. He wasn't like us in *every* respect, of course – for example, he outranked us, by being first among all of God's creatures. But if a dividing line had to be drawn between God and his creation, then Jesus Christ was quite definitely on the creation side of that line. Admittedly, the New Testament used language about Jesus which was difficult to square with this – for example, it referred to him as 'Son of God'. However, according to Arius, this was just a courtesy title. It was a polite way of talking about Jesus.

Arius' main opponent was Athanasius. We know little of his life and his early career. For political reasons, Athanasius became very isolated, and at one point even seemed to be entirely on his own. He was outmanoeuvred by his opponents. He ended up in the political wilderness. But he felt that it was right to keep going. Even if it was Athanasius against the world, he felt that nothing less than the gospel was at stake. He kept going, and in the end saw his perseverance justified. Despite his political isolation, he won the argument. His political restoration soon followed. Athanasius is a constant reminder of the importance of perseverance, when we believe the gospel is at stake and that the New Testament is on our side.

In the end, however, it's the arguments that Athanasius used that are still important today. The Arian controversy gets played over and over again, in student debates, in church meetings, and in theological faculties. People like to feel reassured that the doctrine of the incarnation is right, and not just some outmoded idea dating from centuries ago, which we can throw out of the window in the modern period. Two of Athanasius' arguments are of especial importance.

First, Athanasius makes the point that it is only God who can save. God, and God alone, can break the power of sin, and bring us to eternal life. In doing this, Athanasius takes up a great Old Testament tradition (see, for example, Is. 45:21–2). There is no point in looking to horses, armies, princes or any worldly authorities for salvation: God alone can save. Athanasius builds his argument on this important premise. No creature can save another creature – only the creator can redeem his creation.

Having emphasized that it is God alone who can save,

Athanasius then makes the logical move which Arius found difficult to counter. The New Testament regards Jesus as Saviour. New Testament texts making this suggestion would include Matthew 1:21 (which speaks of Jesus saving his people from their sins), Luke 2:11 (the famous Christmas message of the angels: 'Today in the town of David a Saviour has been born to you'), Acts 4:12 (which affirms that salvation comes through Jesus) and Hebrews 2:10 (which calls Jesus the 'author of salvation'). According to the New Testament, it is *Jesus* who is the Saviour. Yet, as Athanasius emphasized, only God can save. So how are we to make sense of this?

The only possible solution, Athanasius argues, is to accept that Jesus is God incarnate. The logic of his argument goes something like this:

Only God can save.
Jesus saves.
Therefore Jesus is God.

This sort of logic seems to underlie some New Testament passages. For example, Titus 1:3–4 speaks of 'God our Saviour' at one point, and 'Christ Jesus our Saviour' at another. Now Athanasius is able to strengthen his argument by pointing out that no creature can save another creature. Salvation involves divine intervention. Athanasius thus draws out the meaning of John 1:14 by arguing that the 'word became flesh': in other words, God entered into our human situation, in order to change it. To use Athanasius' own words: 'God became man so that we might become like God.' If Jesus was just a creature like the rest of us, he'd be part of the problem, rather than its solution!

The second point that Athanasius makes is that Christians worship and pray to Jesus. By Athanasius' time in the fourth century, these were standard features of the way in which public worship took place. In the New Testament itself, there is ample evidence that both these practices were well established within a remarkably short time of the resurrection. For example, Acts 7:59 records that Stephen prayed to Jesus. Christians are defined in 1 Corinthians

1:2 as 'those who call on the name of our Lord Jesus'. The phrase 'call on' comes from the Old Testament, where it is regularly used to denote 'worship and prayer offered to God' (see Gen. 4:26; 13:4; Ps. 105:1; Je. 10:25; Joel 2:32). And the evidence we have from the early second century suggests that the Christian practice of praying to and worshipping Jesus was used as a way of identifying Christians. There is a famous letter from Pliny, dating from about 115, in which he describes Christians as singing to 'Christ as God'.

Athanasius makes one very simple and powerful point: if Jesus is just a man then Christians are guilty of worshipping a creature! Everyone knows that Christians are totally forbidden to worship anyone or anything except God himself. And if Jesus is just a human being, then they are guilty of worshipping a creature, when they ought to be worshipping the creator. Arius seemed to be guilty of making nonsense of the way in which Christians prayed and worshipped. Their worship had degenerated into idolatry, according to Arius. Athanasius, however, disagreed. Christians were right to worship and adore Jesus Christ, because by doing so, they were recognizing him for what he was (and is!) – God incarnate.

The Arian controversy eventually resulted in what is sometimes called the 'Chalcedonian Definition' (451) – the assertion that Jesus is true God and true man. But this wasn't some dogmatic assertion, laid down by an authoritarian committee who wanted to repress discussion of the question! It was the summary of a centuries-long debate. Many of us have been in a group discussion, or in a committee meeting, where an issue is debated endlessly, with much the same points being raised over and over again. And eventually, someone has to sum up the debate. Its outcome has to be judged. In many ways, the Christian insistence upon the divinity of Jesus Christ may be regarded as passing judgment on the great debate concerning the identity and significance of Jesus, in which the two ideas of Athanasius we've looked at played an important part.

But that debate isn't just a matter of history, which we

21

can forget about in the modern period. For every generation is faced with exactly the same question: who is Jesus Christ? And why is he so important? And Christians are going to want to explain why Jesus is of crucial importance to the human race. The divinity of Jesus is an essential part of that explanation. But the divinity of Jesus is something that we need to be able to defend. Many critics of Christianity will want to insist that Jesus is just another human being, just another religious teacher. The arguments used by Athanasius are still helpful, as we seek to explain and defend the relevance of Jesus to the modern age.

For Further Reading

Gerald Bray, *Creeds, Councils and Christ*, pp. 104–13. An excellent summary of the main points of debate in the discussion of the divinity of Jesus.

Hans von Campenhausen, *The Fathers of the Greek Church*, pp. 69–83. A valuable sketch of the career of Athanasius, as well as an introduction to his basic ideas.

Henry Chadwick, *The Early Church*, pp. 133–51. A readable and informed account of the course of the controversy between Arius and Athanasius, with helpful clarification of the political intrigue accompanying it.

Aloys Grillmeier, *Christ in Christian Tradition*, pp. 302–28. A detailed study of Athanasius' views on the identity and significance of Jesus. Difficult reading: recommended only for those wishing to pursue this subject in depth.

R. P. C. Hanson, *In Search of the Christian Doctrine of God*. A detailed survey of the issues, personalities and problems of the Arian controversy. Strictly for the enthusiast.

CHAPTER TWO

AUGUSTINE OF HIPPO:

The Grace of God

IN the fourth century, the Roman Empire embraced most of the western Mediterranean coastline, including modern-day Algeria. The Christian faith had become strongly established in this area, strengthened by the witness of martyrs such as Cyprian of Carthage. Although generally regarded as something of a backwater by most educated people, it was Roman North Africa which would give the Christian church one of its most important thinkers in the two thousand years of its history. On 13 November 354, a child was born in the town of Thagaste, now known as Souk-Ahras. His parents were probably north Africans who were entitled to Roman citizenship; they were certainly poor. His name was Augustine.

It soon became clear that Augustine was clever, and likely to get on in the world. Inevitably, this meant leaving the family home, and going to a centre of education and learning. His father developed the idea of sending him to Carthage, the great university town of north Africa. Augustine's mother, Monica, was an enthusiastic Christian, who dearly wanted her son to share her faith. Unfortunately, she couldn't handle the questions Augustine wrestled with in his youth. Gradually, Augustine began to become alienated from Christianity. He felt it lacked intellectual respectability.

Augustine went to Carthage to further his studies. The key to a successful legal career was a firm grasp of rhetoric and the Latin language. Augustine soon discovered he was good at both, and exulted in his success. His pursuits, however, extended beyond the purely academic: like young students today, he wanted to explore, to test his limits, to be free, to be able to fall in love. Augustine later recalled how freely he indulged himself sensually once he was no longer restricted by his parents. He took a mistress within a year of his arrival, and was soon father to a son (born in 372, when Augustine was eighteen).

North Africa, however, was home to a religious sect, known as the Manichees. Shortly after the birth of his son, Augustine became involved with this sect. The sect taught a religion which seemed similar to Christianity at certain points. Jesus Christ, for example, was regarded as a good teacher, worth listening to. At other points, however, it had little to do with the gospel, teaching that the God of the Old Testament was malicious and evil, having nothing to do with the God of the New Testament. It was the God of the Old Testament who was responsible for all the evil and suffering of the world. The Old Testament, therefore, was irrelevant to Christians, as it concerned a God inferior to that of the New.

In many ways, the Manichees were like some of the new religious movements which have appeared in North America and western Europe in recent decades. They made enormous demands for commitment on the part of their converts. For example, they frequently demanded that their followers were vegetarian, and that they took a vow of poverty and celibacy. They taught a very simple religious message, which seemed similar to Christianity – yet was in reality profoundly different. Most people, however, knew so little about Christianity that they could not tell the difference.

Augustine found this sect enormously attractive, remaining a member for the next nine years. His mother was horrified, and told her son never to come home again. She approached a local bishop for advice on how to cope with her son. He suggested that she leave Augustine alone, so that he could come to his senses. Monica found this advice unbearable. It seemed to amount to abandoning her son to an unknown fate.

Meanwhile, Augustine's career was going well. In 377,

he won a rhetorical contest presided over by the proconsul of Africa. He even converted some of his friends to Manichaeism. He accepted a teaching post at Carthage, seeing in this a useful stepping stone to higher things at Rome itself. It was only a matter of time before he could begin to climb the ladder that led to important imperial administrative jobs in Rome. He might even become governor of a Roman province. His mother asked him not to go to Rome, which she regarded as a flesh-pot worse than Carthage. In 383 Augustine told his mother he was going to see a friend off at the port: in fact, he boarded a ship and sailed to Rome, taking his mistress with him.

Underneath the veneer of success, however, Augustine was having doubts about the sect he had joined. He heard some Christians making criticisms of its ideas in Carthage, and found these criticisms convincing. The Manichees offered him no satisfactory answers. He began to become aware of spiritual restlessness. He was asking questions which were not being answered. However, he saw no reason to let his Manichaean colleagues know of his doubts. On arriving at Rome, he got in touch with some local sect members. One of them had contacts in the right places, and through his influence Augustine was soon offered the job of Public Orator in the major northern Italian city of Milan.

On his arrival at Milan, Augustine discovered that the local Christian bishop had a reputation as a splendid orator. He decided to find out whether the reputation was merited. Each Sunday, he slipped into the cathedral and listened to the bishop preach. Initially, he took a purely professional interest in the sermons as pieces of splendid oratory: what orator can resist picking up tips, unacknowledged, from another? But gradually, their content began to take hold of him. His doubts concerning Manichaeism increased and an interest in Christianity began to develop. 'I had yet to discover that it taught the truth,' he later remarked, 'but I did discover that it did not teach the things I had accused it of.'

He began to go through a spiritual crisis. He broke off his relationship with his mistress – a relationship which had lasted fifteen years, and given every appearance of stability to his colleagues. Manichaeism no longer had any attraction for Augustine: however, something prevented him from committing himself to Christianity. Something was holding him back; there was a block to his spiritual development. Yet the pressure was building up. Augustine had long been attracted to the writings of the author Marius Victorinus: he now discovered that this writer had become a Christian late in life. A visitor to Augustine's residence told him of how Victorinus had been converted by studying the Scriptures, and had insisted on going to church and making a public declaration of faith. The visitor relished the story as a superb piece of gossip; for Augustine, however, it seemed to be the voice of God addressing him in secret.

The crisis came soon afterwards. Augustine found himself wanting to break with his past, and begin a new relationship with Jesus Christ. He heard reports of others doing this, and wished he could do the same himself. But somehow, the stimulus never came. In his autobiography, Augustine recounts how in August 386 he sat under a fig tree in the garden of his house at Milan, and asked God how much longer this could go on. Why couldn't he set aside his baseness here and now? As if by answer, he heard some children playing in a neighbouring garden. They were singing as they played, and the words they sang were, 'Take up and read! Take up and read!' Augustine rushed indoors, opened his New Testament at random, and read the verses which stood out from the page: 'Clothe yourselves with the Lord Jesus Christ, and do not think about how to gratify the desires of your lower nature' (Rom. 13:14). He closed the book, and told his friends he had become a Christian.

How do we know all this? Augustine wrote an autobiography, known as *The Confessions*, in which he describes the chain of events leading up to his conversion. One of the most interesting features of this work is the way in which Augustine recognizes that God was working in his life long before his conversion, gradually preparing the way for this great event. Time and time again, Augustine interrupts his account of his career to praise God for the way in which his hand has been at work in his life.

Within ten years, Augustine was a bishop in north Africa, and had become one of the most influential thinkers that Christianity has ever produced. His massive talent was now directed towards the work of the gospel, rather than his own career in the Roman administration. In this chapter, we are going to look at Augustine's views on the grace of God, widely regarded as one of his most important contributions to Christian thought. Through Augustine, Paul's teaching on sin and grace began to be recovered by a church which had come close to losing sight of it.

The debate involving Augustine which concerns us here is known as the Pelagian controversy. This broke out at the beginning of the fifth century, and centred on Pelagius, who had recently arrived at Rome from Britain (probably Scotland). Pelagius was a moral reformer, who felt (apparently with some justification) that Christianity at Rome had become rather lax. He began a programme of reform, laying considerable stress on the human ability to do good.

One day, however, Pelagius overheard someone reading aloud Augustine's *Confessions*. The passage being read concerned Augustine's sense of being totally dependent upon the mercy of God. 'My whole hope is only in your mercy. Give what you command, and command what you will.' Pelagius was shocked by these words. They seemed to be saying that we were dependent on God, and not on ourselves. His whole programme of moral reform seemed to be at stake. He began to challenge Augustine. The debate was long and not a little confused. After all, Pelagius was based at Rome, while Augustine was in north Africa – and communications were not particularly satisfactory in those days. However, despite these difficulties, the main lines of the controversy are clear, and are still of enormous interest and importance.

Pelagius asserted that we are completely free in all our actions. We are not influenced by hidden forces, nor are we restricted by powers which lie beyond our control. We are the masters of our own destiny. If we are told to stop sinning, we can stop sinning. Sin is something which we can and must resist. God has given us the Ten Commandments and the example of Jesus Christ, and it's up to us to live according to them. According to Pelagius, any imperfection in human nature which might stop us acting morally would reflect badly on God. After all, God made us – to say that there's something wrong with human nature means that God didn't create us particularly well. It's insulting to God, as well as to us, to suggest that there's some inbuilt fault in human nature.

Augustine, however, realized that the New Testament, especially the writings of Paul, seemed to be saying something rather different. For Augustine, Pelagius' views on human nature were dangerously naive, and bore little relation to either the New Testament teaching or to human experience. So Augustine responded to Pelagius by giving a detailed exposition of the New Testament understanding of human nature, sin and divine grace, which came to be recognized as masterly. We'll look at his ideas on human nature first.

There's something wrong with human nature. Augustine's basic belief is that human nature, although created without any problems, is contaminated by sin as a result of the Fall. In other words, there's a flaw in human nature. This flaw wasn't there when God created us. The Genesis creation accounts make it abundantly clear that God created us well. But then something happened – something which introduced a flaw into human nature. Augustine refers to this as the Fall, meaning the disobedience of Adam – something which wasn't God's fault. As a result of this, human nature just isn't capable of doing the sorts of things Pelagius feels it ought to. There is a bias towards sin and away from God in our human nature, as a result of the Fall. Fallen human beings have a built-in tendency to sin.

To explain this point, Augustine uses a helpful analogy. Consider a pair of scales, with two balance pans. One balance pan represents good, and the other evil. If the pans are properly balanced, the arguments in favour of doing good or doing evil could be weighed, and a proper conclusion drawn. The parallel with the human free will is obvious: we weigh up the arguments in favour of doing good and evil, and act accordingly. But what, asks Augustine, if the balance pans are loaded? What happens if someone puts several heavy weights in the balance pan on the side of evil? The scales will still work, but they are seriously biased towards making an evil decision. Augustine argues that this is exactly what has happened to humanity through sin. The human free will is biased towards evil. It really exists, and really can make decisions – just as the loaded scales still work. But instead of giving a balanced judgment, there's a serious bias towards evil.

One of the more impressive features of Augustine's account of the influence of sin upon the human free will is that it is so obviously true to experience. All of us have experienced being torn between *knowing* that something is good, and *not being able or willing to do it*. It is this tension which Paul recognizes: 'What I do is not the good I want to do; no, the evil I do not want to do – this is what I keep on doing' (Rom. 7:19). This inbuilt human tendency to want to do what is wrong is reflected in the famous story about a visitor to a European monastery. This visitor was shown to his room by the monks. They then told him that he could do anything he liked – providing he didn't look out of one of the windows. It was high up on a wall, far above eye level. Eventually, he was unable to control his curiosity. Placing a chair below the window, he was able to reach far enough up to see out of of this forbidden window – and was horrified to find the monks assembled there, awaiting his inevitable appearance. 'They always look out!' was their final word, as they went away laughing.

The basic point Augustine makes is that we have no control over the fact that we are sinful. It is something which contaminates our lives from birth, and dominates our lives thereafter. He uses the term 'original sin' to refer to this inbuilt human problem. We are born alienated from God, and need to be born all over again if we are to have a full relationship with God. Sin is a state over which we have no decisive control. We could say that Augustine understands humanity to be born with a sinful disposition as part of human nature, with an inherent bias towards acts of sinning. Sin causes sins: the *state* of sinfulness causes *individual acts of sin*. So how are we to think of sin? Augustine suggests three ways of thinking about original sin as a 'disease', as a 'power' and as 'guilt'.

First, think of sin as an hereditary disease, which is passed down from one generation to another. As we saw above, this disease weakens humanity, and cannot be cured by human agency. Christ is thus the divine physician, by whose 'wounds we are healed' (Is. 53:5), and salvation is understood in medical terms. We are healed by the grace of God, so that our minds may recognize God and our wills may respond to him.

Second, think of sin as a power which holds us captive, and from whose grip we are unable to break free by ourselves. The human free will is captivated by the power of sin, and may only be liberated by grace. Christ is thus seen as the liberator, the source of the grace which breaks the power of sin.

Third, think of sin as a legal idea – guilt – which is passed down from one generation to another. In a society which placed a high value on law, such as the later Roman Empire, in which Augustine lived and worked, this was regarded as a particularly helpful way of understanding sin. Christ thus comes to bring forgiveness and pardon.

These ways of thinking about sin have proved very helpful, and you have probably come across them already. You may even know the following lines in A. M. Toplady's famous hymn *Rock of Ages*:

> Let the water and the blood,
> From thy riven side which flowed,
> Be of sin the double cure,
> Cleanse me from its guilt and power.

The 'double cure' of sin refers to the need for sin to be forgiven, and its power to be broken – note the appeal to the death of Christ as the source of this cure. Or you may know these lines from the famous hymn by Charles Wesley, *O for a thousand tongues, to sing*:

> He breaks the power of cancelled sin,
> He sets the prisoner free;
> His blood can make the foulest clean,
> His blood availed for me.

The reference to breaking 'the power of cancelled sin' is particularly important, bringing together the ideas of liberation from the *power* of sin and *forgiveness* of its guilt – 'cancelled sin' is forgiven sin.

Augustine develops an idea already found in the New Testament, especially Romans. The Law is able to tell us what we ought to do – but it doesn't help us to do what is good. There is something about human nature that inclines it to do things it knows to be wrong. The Law can tell us what's wrong, identifying sin, but is powerless to help us to avoid it (Rom. 7:7–20). We need help from outside if we are to act on the knowledge of what sin is. But who or what can help us? For Paul, the answer is provided by the gospel, the good news of Jesus Christ. God himself has intervened to help us, giving us the means by which we can not only identify sin, but also break free from its stranglehold. 'Who will rescue me from this body of death? Thanks be to God – through Jesus Christ our Lord!' (Rom. 7:24–5).

Augustine develops this basic idea, arguing that we are trapped through sin, and are unable to break free from its power. Through the Law, we are able to identify sin. Yet it still exercises influence over us. It is like some mysterious fascinating force, attracting us like a magnet. Identifying the enemy is only the beginning of the battle. For Augustine, we are unequal to the struggle. If we were left on our own, we would fail miserably. We would just become more deeply embedded in our situation.

Have you ever watched a truck get stuck in mud? The more the driver accelerates, the more deeply the truck gets stuck. All the effort which is meant to get the truck out of the mud just makes the hole deeper instead, so that the situation gets worse rather than better. What is needed is for someone outside the situation, who isn't trapped in the mud, to come and get it out.

Or again, think of yourself as being in prison. Being told that you're in prison is helpful – but it doesn't get you out! It clarifies your situation for you, and helps you think through how you might get out of that situation. But the mere knowledge that you're in jail isn't enough to set you free. Someone has to get you out. They might blast the jail open, or they might just turn a key in the door lock – but either way, someone else has intervened to set you free.

Pelagius argues that we are not trapped in any situation, and don't need anybody else to help us out. We are free! In many ways, Pelagius resembles the subject of William Ernest Henley's poem *Invictus*, a great favourite with the Victorians:

> It matters not how strait the gate,
> How charged with punishment the scroll,
> I am the master of my fate:
> I am the captain of my soul!

Augustine suggests that the only way we are ever likely to get free is by being realistic about our situation. He argues that sin traps humanity within nature, allowing us freedom within this sphere of activity – but preventing us from breaking free from it to encounter and respond to the living God. We are like trucks stuck in the mud – someone has to come and pull us out. Through grace, God enables us to break free from the limitations of our natural condition, and recognize and respond to his gracious call. For Augustine, we are blind to God, and our eyes must be opened by grace; we are deaf to his word, and our ears must be opened in the same way.

What is grace? It has been explained as 'God's Riches At Christ's Expense', a very helpful way of beginning to think about grace. Augustine uses two helpful images to help us think about grace. First, grace is understood as the *liberator* of human nature. It's like a breakdown truck, which arrives to pull someone out of the mud. It's like a key, which unlocks the door of a prison cell. To go back to the scales analogy, grace removes the weights loading the scales towards evil, and allows us to recognize the full weight of the case for choosing God. Thus Augustine is able to argue that grace, far from abolishing or compromising the human free will, actually establishes it.

Second, grace is understood as the *healer* of human nature. One of Augustine's favourite analogies for the church is that of a hospital, full of sick people. Christians are those who recognize that they are ill, and seek the assistance of a physician, in order that they may be healed. Thus Augustine appeals to the parable of the good Samaritan (Lk. 10:30–34), in suggesting that human nature is like the man who was left for dead by the roadside, until he was rescued and healed by the Samaritan (representing Christ as redeemer, according to Augustine). On the basis of illustrations such as these, Augustine argues that the human free will is unhealthy, and needs healing. Once more, grace is understood as establishing, rather than destroying, human free will, as the obstacles which prevent the free will from functioning properly are removed.

Augustine uses many other analogies to explain the problem of human sin, to help us understand the idea of grace better. An analogy which Augustine doesn't use may also prove helpful. Let's suppose you are walking through a city street one day, when you're stopped by a young man. He offers you a white powder. He tells you it's great. Take this, and you'll have marvellous experiences. You'll experience a whole new dimension to life. You are tempted. What harm can come out of it? It's only a white powder, after all. (Can you see the parallels with Gn. 3?) And you give in, buying a packet of the powder, anxiously looking round to see if you're being watched.

When you get home, you snort the powder, and think it's great. Then you make the dreadful discovery – you can't break the habit. You're hooked. You need more and more of this white powder. You're hooked. You're trapped. Your whole life begins to centre on getting further supplies of cocaine. It doesn't help you to be told that you're hooked – you know that. It doesn't help you to be told that you've made a big mistake – you know that. What you need is someone to break the habit for you. You need help. You're like the man left for dead on the road from Jerusalem to Jericho, unable to help himself.

This is a good way of thinking of the human predicament, according to both Paul and Augustine. Like people hooked on cocaine, we are trapped by sin. We can't help ourselves to break free, to turn away from sin and discover the love of God. So is there no hope for us? Is there no way in which we can break free from this situation? Both Paul and Augustine exult in the fact that God has graciously intervened in our situation, sending Jesus Christ into the world to break the power of sin, to set us free from it. The gospel declares that we are sinners, and then offers us the means to break the power of sin – by faith in Jesus Christ.

Augustine's understanding of Christianity is dominated by the thought of the grace of God. Perhaps his favourite text is 'Apart from me, you can do nothing' (Jn. 15:5). Christ's death and resurrection break the power of sin, and cancel its guilt. Christ is the second Adam, the one who came to restore us to fellowship with God and empower us to keep the Law. As Augustine himself puts it, 'Grace is not just knowledge of the divine law or our own nature or the forgiveness of sins. It is something which is given to us through our Lord Jesus Christ so that by it the law may be fulfilled, nature delivered and sin defeated.'

Why is this emphasis on the grace of God so important? Two points are worth thinking about. First, grace means we are not totally dependent on our own resources. It affirms that God does not leave us alone, as we are confronted with the challenges and opportunities of the Christian life. Just as God acted to free us from the power of sin and forgive its guilt, so he is with us throughout our Christian lives. At one point, Paul relates how he found himself in a situation of utter helplessness, in which he became acutely aware of his own weakness. He recalls how he took comfort from the Lord's words, 'My grace is sufficient for you, for my power is made perfect in weakness' (2 Cor. 12:9).

Second, grace means that no-one is beyond the reach of

God's love. Paul and Augustine were both acutely aware of this fact. Paul was the man who persecuted the church of God, approving of the death of Stephen (Acts 8:1). He might have seemed to lie beyond the reach of the love and power of God. But, as the story of the journey on the road to Damascus shows, God is able to work even in the lives of the most unlikely people. 'For I am the least of the apostles and do not even deserve to be called an apostle, because I persecuted the church of God. But by the grace of God I am what I am, and his grace to me was not without effect' (1 Cor. 15:9–10).

Augustine was also aware of how amazing the grace of God could be. As he set sail for Rome to escape his mother, he seemed to be turning his back on his mother's Christian faith. Yet he went into a situation in which he encountered God, and was totally transformed by the experience. Again, Augustine appears to have led a profligate life as a student, with little interest in the Christian faith and considerable interest in the good things of life. But as he grew older, having tasted the delights of youth, he found that he was profoundly unsatisfied. He longed for something more satisfying, something deeper – and found these longings satisfied by the Christian faith. This is an important point to bear in mind within student Christian circles: many young people who show no interest in, or even turn their backs upon, Christianity may rediscover its vitality later in life. The example of Augustine reminds us never to give up hope.

For Further Reading

For excellent accounts of Augustine's life and ministry, including his conversion and the Pelagian controversy, see: Gerald Bonner, *Augustine of Hippo: Life and Controversies*.

Peter Brown, *Augustine of Hippo: A Biography*.

Henry Chadwick, *Augustine*, is especially helpful – and it's short!

CHAPTER THREE

ANSELM OF CANTERBURY:

The Death of Christ

LIKE a curtain at the end of the first act of a play, so the Dark Ages descended upon Europe. The collapse of the Roman Empire and the barbarian invasions marked the beginning of a difficult period in European history. The Dark Ages would lift towards the end of the eleventh century. Until then, Christian thinkers found themselves more concerned with survival than anything else! It was a period of political instability and anxiety. Nevertheless, it was also a period of faith, as Christianity continued its spread. Missionaries moved northwards and westwards, ensuring that even in the Dark Ages the light of Christ shone.

There are some powerful Christian writings from this period. Many students of English literature have come across the famous Anglo-Saxon poem, known as *The Dream of the Rood* – 'rood' is the Old English word for 'cross'. We don't know exactly when it was written, although most scholars think it dates from about 750. It is a marvellous poem, which is basically a meditation on the death of Jesus on the cross. The poet tells of how he fell asleep, and dreamed about a tree. The tree tells its story: how it once grew in a forest, but was one day chopped down, and taken to a hill. After the tree had been erected on the hill, a young hero was nailed to it. The tree shuddered as the nails were hammered home, and was drenched with the blood which poured from his wounds. This, reflects the poet, is the enormous cost of the redemption of humanity. This is how much God loved the world, The cost of redemption is astonishingly high – yet it is real redemption. The image of the suffering Christ, nailed to the cross, lingers as the poem draws to its end. It reminds us of the full extent of God's love.

The central figure of this chapter was born somewhat later, as the Dark Ages began to lift from Europe. Anselm was born in in northern Italy in 1033, the son of a Lombard nobleman. As a young man, Anselm decided to leave his parents' home, and began to travel northwards into France, eventually settling down in Normandy. The place at which he settled is nowadays known as Le Bec-Hellouin. Hellouin was a Norman knight who was so interested in Christianity that he turned his estate into a monastery. The monastery was called Le Bec, which soon established itself as a centre of learning and faith. It was at this monastery that Anselm eventually arrived, attracted by the reputation of its abbot at the time, Lanfranc.

In 1066, William the Conqueror invaded England, and began to install Normans in positions of importance throughout the country. William invited Lanfranc to come to England, and become Archbishop of Canterbury. Anselm became abbot in Lanfranc's place, and remained in this position for fifteen years. While on a visit to England, Anselm was made Archbishop of Canterbury by King William II. He died in 1109, aged seventy-five, after a period of fifteen years which witnessed considerable tension between the English church and the Norman kings. In fact, Anselm was probably out of England more than in it during the period, as he was often exiled by William II and Henry I.

Anselm wrote a number of works. One of these, entitled *Why God became Man*, was written while visiting Italy in 1098. It's often referred to by its Latin title, *Cur Deus homo*. In this work, Anselm deals at length with the question of the meaning of the death of Christ. What he says is still worth hearing.

The central problem Anselm wrestles with was this: why did God have to redeem us through the death of Christ on the cross? Why couldn't he have done something much simpler? For example, why could he not have simply declared sin to be forgiven and forgotten? After all, God is merciful – why can't he just show that mercy by over-looking sin, or telling us that it doesn't matter? The answer he gave to this problem was enormously stimulating, and very important.

Anselm points out that there are many things that can be said about God. For example, he is merciful; he is wise; he is just. All of these can be determined without any difficulty from Scripture. But these qualities, or attributes, of God cannot be considered in isolation from each other. God isn't merciful on Mondays and Tuesdays, wise on Wednesdays and Thursdays, and just on Fridays and Saturdays. He is all of these things, all of the time.

This means that we cannot isolate one of God's attributes – like mercy – and treat it on its own, as if that said everything about who God is and what he is like. God is indeed merciful – but he is also wise and just. With this in mind, let's consider the question: why can't God just forgive and forget sin? After all, he's merciful, isn't he? And what could be more merciful than that?

Anselm agrees that God is merciful. After all, it is God's mercy which made him want to redeem us in the first place. But God's justice and wisdom aren't suspended. Let's put Anselm's insight in a rather formal way: God's attributes must coexist within the limiting conditions they impose upon one another. Or, to put this in plain English, one of God's attributes (such as his mercy) doesn't overrule the others (such as his justice) – they are all involved in determining the way in which God deals with us.

Anselm's discussion could be summarized like this. God's mercy and his justice are both involved in the redemption of humanity. God's tender mercy makes him want to redeem us in the first place; his justice determines the way in which he redeems us. Both mercy and justice are thus involved in redemption – but they are involved in different ways. God's mercy leads to the *decision* to redeem; God's justice leads to the particular *method* of redemption chosen. Neither God's mercy nor his justice are suspended – they are both in operation. Now if God just declared that sin was forgiven, his mercy would indeed be satisfied – but what about his justice? God's implacable hostility to sin would be compromised. God would give the impression of having done some shady deal, by which his own principles were compromised.

Do you remember the row about President Reagan's arms deal with Iran? Ronald Reagan – perhaps the most popular president of the United States in recent years – constantly affirmed his total opposition to terrorism. Terrorists (and President Reagan regarded Iran as a terrorist nation) should be isolated. They should be quarantined. Nobody should do any deals with them. Then it turned out that President Reagan had authorized the sale of military equipment to Iran. The same man who had used all his moral authority to oppose dealing with Iran was seen to have compromised his own principles. He was being inconsistent. Some even suggested that he was being dishonest. His popularity slumped. The moral of this incident is clear: if you condemn something, don't compromise your principles by doing that thing yourself!

It is obvious how this principle applies to God and the redemption of humanity. As Scripture makes abundantly clear, God is totally opposed to sin. He loves the sinner, certainly – but the sin, he detests. If God were to be seen to act in such a way as to condone sin, his integrity would be compromised. If God were to pretend that sin didn't really matter, the scriptural condemnations of sin would be seen to be hollow. If God can act in such a way as to tolerate sin, failing to condemn it, why should we not behave in the same way? It is not enough that God *is* just – he must be *seen* to act in a just manner. The redemption of the world thus becomes a test case. Will God act publicly in the righteous manner that his condemnations of sin suggest? Or will he continue to condemn sin, while doing some kind of deal with it behind our backs, along the lines of Ronald Reagan and Iran?

Now Ronald Reagan was able to explain his action in dealing with Iran along the following lines: there were American hostages held by groups sympathetic to Iran. By doing a deal with Iran, it would be possible to speed up the release of these hostages. The end thus justified the means.

But, as the opinion polls soon made clear, the American public was not impressed. Both the end *and the means* had to be consistent with moral principles. The redemption of the world is admirable, as an end or goal – but the means by which this is attained must be seen to be principled. God has to demonstrate publicly his justice, his determination to deal with sin firmly and fairly, in the way in which he redeems the world.

Let Anselm make his central point in his own words:

> Let us consider whether it is right for God to forgive sins by mercy alone, without any payment of the honour taken from him ... To remit sin in this way is nothing other than not punishing it. And since it is not right to cancel sin without compensation or punishment, it follows that if it isn't punished, then it's left unforgiven. ... And another thing. If sin isn't punished, it follows that God doesn't make any distinction between the guilty and the non-guilty, which is unthinkable.

So God can't just forgive and forget sin, as if it never happened. God maintains his integrity throughout the whole work of redemption. But why did God choose to redeem the world through the death of Jesus? How does this uphold God's justice? Let's follow Anselm's argument through, and see how he combines God's mercy and justice.

Why did God create us in the first place? According to Anselm, God created us in order to be able to bring us to eternal life, and grant us blessedness. This, however, is conditional: it depends upon total obedience to God. The promise of eternal life is real; there is a condition attached, however. On account of human sin, unfortunately, it is impossible for us to meet this condition. Human sin makes it impossible for us to be obedient to God. We can't meet the basic precondition for eternal life. In addition to that, our sin gives offence to God. Therefore, either God's purpose in creating us has been frustrated, or there must be some way round the problem.

40

Anselm declares that the gospel is concerned with the solution of this problem.

Anselm then develops his ideas using some legal imagery. Of particular importance is the idea of *satisfaction*. Suppose you lived in the early feudal period, and got involved in a dispute with some local dignitary – for example, the lord of the manor. You might have stolen an egg, for example. If you were caught, feudal law demanded that two things happen. First, you had to restore the situation. You would have to return the egg. But in addition to this, you had to compensate your victim for the offence given. A satisfaction was required. The more serious the offence, the greater the compensation you were obliged to pay.

Anselm thus builds up to the central problem of redemption. Redemption is only possible if satisfaction is made for human sin. But, on account of human sin, we are unable to make this satisfaction. We are unable to redeem ourselves. It is not just that we are incapable of the basic obedience demanded of us by God, if we are to receive eternal life – we are unable to compensate for the offence given by our disobedience. But – and here Anselm's argument reaches its crucial point – God himself could make the necessary satisfaction.

We could state Anselm's argument like this.

1. Human beings have an obligation, but not an ability, to make the satisfaction required if God is to grant us eternal life.
2. God himself has no obligation to make this satisfaction; however, he has the ability to make this satisfaction.
3. Therefore, Anselm concludes, if God became man, the result would be a God-man who has both the obligation and the ability to restore the situation, and allow us to regain eternal life.

Anselm thus argues that the incarnation – that is, God becoming man – is a just solution of the problem of the redemption of the world. And so Anselm demonstrates that the incarnation makes a lot of sense. If God is really

41

going to redeem us, he's got to come among us, as a human being.

Anselm's argument continues from this point, stressing that Christ's obedience compensates for our disobedience. If Christ were just a man, sharing our human condition, redemption would be impossible; his death would not have any particular value. However, because he is none other than God incarnate, he is able to achieve the satisfaction necessary for human sin, thus restoring the possibility of eternal life. Christ's obedience, culminating in his death on the cross, makes up for our disobedience. Here, Anselm is exploring one of Paul's characteristic ideas, in which the disobedience of Adam is contrasted with the obedience of Christ: 'For just as through the disobedience of the one man the many were made sinners, so also through the obedience of the one man the many will be made righteous' (Rom. 5:19).

Obviously, there are many critical questions which need to be asked about Anselm's understanding of the death of Christ. For example, he does tend to treat God as if he is lord of the manor, someone who is very easily offended – and many modern readers find this rather feudal. Of course, Anselm could reply that he was just doing what every good preacher does – using contemporary analogies to make theological points. If you live in a feudal age, you use feudal analogies. Nevertheless, some points are made very forcefully and very persuasively. God does not use questionable means in our redemption; sin requires to be taken seriously.

God doesn't just say something like 'Never mind – we'll pretend that sin never happened.' Even we would find that a shockingly superficial attitude. No – God deals with sin at its root, insisting that it is taken seriously, and *really* forgiven. And for those of us who know how real sin can be, it is vital that we know that our real sins are really forgiven. We need to know that our sins really have been cancelled and forgiven, so that we can rest secure with the God who loves us. Forgiveness is shown to be a very costly matter. But the cost of our redemption also reminds us of how precious we are to God. We must mean something to God, if he goes to such lengths to forgive us, and restore us to fellowship with him.

One of Anselm's central ideas is that sin is like serious debt. This idea has become increasingly familiar in the modern period. One of the major problems of western society in the final decades of the twentieth century is excess credit. Credit card companies offer people the possibility of buying items on credit which otherwise would be beyond their means. As a result many people gradually fall deeply into debt. They owe sums of money which they cannot hope to pay back. There is nothing that they can do to get out of this situation. They are trapped.

As time progresses, the debt becomes worse, as interest and service charges mount up. They lose hope of ever breaking out of their situation. They may try to pretend that the problem doesn't really exist: unfortunately, this doesn't change the situation. A sense of despondency settles over them. Their financial problems exercise power over them, and threaten them. Something that has no life in itself begins to behave as if it were a living and hostile being. If you have never been in this situation, try to think yourself into it. Try to capture the sense of despair and anxiety.

Anselm encourages us to think of our sinful situation as being hopelessly in debt. We cannot pay off our debt ourselves – and yet the debt must be paid if we are to be set free from the baleful influence of sin. God's justice demands that the debt be paid – and God's mercy offers to pay that debt for us. Try to imagine the enormous sense of relief you would feel if someone offered to pay off a crippling debt you had incurred. An enormous load would be lifted from your back; you could walk tall again.

In his writings, Anselm tries to be faithful to the New Testament. Perhaps he is less successful in this than we would like; perhaps he goes too far beyond the New Testament than we feel is appropriate. But he is concerned to do something of permanent importance – to stress that the cross possesses its saving value only on account of the divinity of Christ. If Christ is simply a man, the human race gains nothing from his death. It is on account of the fact that Jesus is none other than God incarnate that his death brings redemption and eternal life. In many ways, Anselm is echoing an important point, made more poetically centuries beforehand in *The Dream of the Rood*:

> This is the tree of glory
> On which God almighty once suffered pain
> For the many sins of humanity, and for the deeds
> Of Adam, long ago.

For Further Reading

Anselm's prayers and meditations, many of which are very moving, are collected together in *The Prayers and Meditations of Saint Anselm*, a Penguin classic.

His *Why God became Man* may be found in *Saint Anselm: Basic Writings*, translated by S. N. Deane, pp. 171–288.

An excellent introduction to the life and work of Anselm may be found in Gillian R. Evans, *Anselm*.

CHAPTER FOUR

THOMAS AQUINAS:
Faith and Reason

AS political stability broke out in western Europe in the twelfth century, a renaissance got under way. A revival of interest in the sciences, the arts and religion became widespread. One of the major centres for this revival was the city and university of Paris, which attracted scholars from throughout Europe as teachers. In its early period, the university of Paris was little more than a collection of schools. Some of the major schools were established on the Ile de la Cité, in the shadow of the great cathedral of Notre Dame, then nearing completion. There are references in the writings of some twelfth-century theologians to the difficulties in studying with all the noise caused by stonemasons building the cathedral! Other schools were established on the left bank of the Seine. One such school was the Collège de la Sorbonne, which eventually achieved such fame that 'the Sorbonne' eventually came to be a shorthand way of referring to the University of Paris. Even in the sixteenth century, Paris was widely recognized as a leading centre for theological and philosophical study, including among its students such names as Erasmus of Rotterdam and John Calvin.

One of the most famous teachers of the University of Paris during the Middle Ages was Thomas Aquinas (c. 1225–1274). Aquinas was born at the castle of Roccasecca in Italy, the youngest son of Count Landulf of Aquino. To judge by his nickname – 'the dumb ox' – he was rather portly. In 1244, while in his late teens, Aquinas decided to join the Dominican Order, also known as the 'Order of

Preachers'. His parents were hostile to this idea: they rather hoped he would become a Benedictine, and perhaps end up as abbot of Monte Cassino, one of the most prestigious positions in the medieval church. His brothers forcibly imprisoned him in one of the family's castles for a year to encourage him to change his mind. Despite this intense opposition from his family, Aquinas eventually got his way, and ended up becoming one of the most important religious thinkers of the Middle Ages. One of his teachers is reported to have said that 'the bellowing of that ox will be heard throughout the world'.

Aquinas began his studies at Paris, before moving to Cologne in 1248. In 1252 he returned to Paris to study theology. Four years later, he was granted permission to teach theology at the university. For the next three years he lectured on Matthew's gospel and began to write the *Summa contra Gentiles*, 'Summary against the Gentiles'. In this major work, Aquinas provided important arguments for the Christian faith for the benefit of missionaries working amongst Muslims and Jews. In 1266, he began to write the most famous of his many writings, usually known by its Latin title, *Summa Theologiae*. (A rough English translation might be 'Everything you wanted to know about theology'!) Aquinas never finished this work. On 6 December 1273, he declared that he could write no longer. 'All that I have written seems like straw to me,' he said. It is possible that he may have had some sort of breakdown, perhaps brought on by overwork. He died on 7 March 1274.

Even in its unfinished form, the *Summa Theologiae* is massive: it has 512 questions, 2,669 articles, and more than 10,000 objections and replies. It is easily available in English translation, and is still an invaluable introduction to many areas of Christian theology. One of these areas stands out as being of especial importance: the relation of faith and reason.

One basic anxiety which you, and many other Christians, may feel concerns the *rationality* of your faith. Have you committed intellectual suicide by becoming a Christian? You may have wondered whether, if you thought about your faith long and hard enough, you would realize that it was complete nonsense? Is there some deep contradiction between faith and reason? For example, take belief in God himself. Is *that* irrational? Or are there reasons for thinking that it makes sense?

This is not to say that the existence of God can be proved. This has always been seen as a matter of faith. Indeed, the Austrian philosopher Ludwig Wittgenstein insisted that nobody ever believed in God on account of an argument. What we are talking about, however, is something rather different. *Given* that you believe in God, can this belief be shown to make sense? You don't come to faith through an argument about the existence of God. But once you *do* come to faith, it makes sense to ask whether this belief is reasonable. Is it internally consistent, for example? Or is there some obvious contradiction involved?

Let's take the case of belief in God. If all the evidence available pointed against the existence of God, it would be rather difficult to sustain that belief! You might feel that you were standing with your back against a brick wall, with all the evidence for the non-existence of God pressing against you. It therefore seems reasonable to ask whether your faith in God makes sense, given whatever evidence is available. You don't expect to be able to prove that God *does* exist – but you can reasonably expect to be able to convince yourself that, given the Christian understanding of who God is and what he is like, your knowledge of the world ties in with belief in his existence. This is the type of argument developed more recently by C. S. Lewis, to whom we'll return later.

Aquinas' contribution to this discussion is of major importance. Although some philosophers seem to think that Aquinas was out to prove the existence of God, this is clearly not the case. In front of me, I have a copy of one of the standard editions of Aquinas' *Summa Theologiae*. It is more than four thousand pages long. His discussion of 'whether God exists' is just over two pages long! So it is fairly obvious that Aquinas did not feel that he was setting out to prove the essential basis of the Christian faith in his discussion of reasons for believing that God existed. It is perfectly clear that his primary reason for believing in the existence of God is God's revelation of himself. Aquinas expects his readers to share his faith in God, not that he will have to prove it to them first. Nevertheless, Aquinas believes that it is proper to identify pointers towards the existence of God, drawn from outside Scripture. After all, Paul seems to suggest this kind of approach (Rom. 1:19–21). Yet these arguments or pointers are *supports*, not *proofs*, for the existence of God.

So what kind of pointers does Aquinas identify? The basic line of thought guiding Aquinas is that the world as we know it mirrors God, as its creator. Just as an artist might sign a painting to identify it as his handiwork, so God has stamped his signature upon his creation. What we observe in the world can be explained on the basis of the existence of God as its creator. He is its first cause, and its designer. God both brought the world into existence, and impressed his image and likeness upon it.

So where might we look in creation to find evidence for the existence of God? For the Psalmist, the starry heavens declare the existence and glory of God (Ps. 19:1–3). For Aquinas, however, it is the ordering of the world which is the most convincing evidence of God's existence and wisdom. This argument, often referred to as the 'argument from design' or the 'teleological argument', has remained of importance ever since. Let's begin by outlining the five arguments (sometimes referred to as the 'Five Ways') that Aquinas identifies as providing pointers to the existence of God.

The first way begins from the observation that things in the world are in motion or change. The world is not static, but is dynamic. Examples of this are easy to list. Rain falls from the sky. Stones roll down valleys. The earth revolves around the sun (a fact, incidentally, unknown to Aquinas). But how did nature come to be in motion? Why isn't it static?

Aquinas argues that everything which moves is moved by something else. For every motion, there is a cause. Things don't just move – they are moved. Now each cause of motion must itself have a cause. And *that* cause must have a cause as well. And so Aquinas argues that there are a whole series of causes of motion lying behind the world as we know it. Now unless there are an infinite number of these causes, Aquinas argues, there must be a single cause right at the origin of the series. From this original cause of motion, all other motion is ultimately derived. This is the origin of the great chain of causality which we see reflected in the way the world behaves. From the fact that things are in motion, Aquinas thus argues for the existence of a single original cause of all this motion – and this, he concludes, is God himself.

The second way begins from the idea of causation. In other words, Aquinas notes the existence of causes and effects in the world. One event (the effect) is explained by the influence of another (the cause). The idea of motion, which we looked at briefly above, is a good example of this cause-and-effect sequence. Using a line of reasoning similar to that used above, Aquinas thus argues that all effects may be traced back to a single original cause – which is God himself.

The third way concerns the existence of contingent beings. In other words, the world contains beings (such as ourselves) which aren't there by necessity. Aquinas contrasts this type of being with a necessary being (one who is there as a matter of necessity). While God is a necessary being, Aquinas argues that we are contingent beings. The fact that we *are* here needs explanation. Why are we here? What happened to bring us into existence?

Aquinas then argues that a being comes into existence because something which already exists brought it into being. In other words, our existence is caused by another being. We are the effects of a series of causation. Tracing this series back to its origin, Aquinas declares that this original cause of being can only be someone whose existence is necessary – in other words, God.

The fourth way begins from human values, such as truth, goodness and nobility. Where do these values come from? What causes them? Aquinas argues that there must be something which is in itself true, good and noble, and that this brings into being our ideas of truth, goodness and nobility. The origin of these ideas, Aquinas suggests, is

God, who is their original cause. A considerably more subtle version of this argument is associated with C. S. Lewis, and will be discussed later in this work (chapter 11).

The final way is the teleological argument itself. Aquinas notes that the world shows obvious traces of intelligent design. Natural processes and objects seem to be adapted with certain definite objectives in mind. They seem to have a purpose. They seem to have been designed. But things don't design themselves: they are caused and designed by someone or something else. Arguing from this observation, Aquinas concludes that the source of this natural ordering must be conceded to be God himself.

It will be obvious that most of Aquinas' arguments are rather similar. Each depends on tracing a causal sequence back to its origin, and identifying this with God. In the end, however, these arguments do not prove the existence of the 'God and Father of our Lord Jesus Christ' (1 Pet. 1:3). They go some way towards suggesting that it is reasonable to believe in a creator of the world, or an intelligent being who is able to cause effects in the world. Nevertheless, a leap of faith is still required. We still have to show that this creator or intelligent being *is* the God whom Christians know, worship and adore. Aquinas' arguments could lead to faith in the existence of a god rather like that favoured by the Greek philosopher Aristotle – an Unmoved Mover, who is distant from and uninvolved in the affairs of his world. Nevertheless, to the Christian reader of Aquinas, his arguments are useful backup material for faith. They don't establish faith in God, but they give this faith some useful support, by showing that it does make some sort of sense.

However, a serious discussion of the rationality of the Christian faith involves far more than showing that the existence of God is reasonable! It involves a careful study of the limits of human reason, as it attempts to wrestle with something which is ultimately far beyond its grasp – the living God. To what extent is reason able to cope with God? If God is above and beyond our world, how can human reason ever hope to make sense of him? How can God ever be described or discussed using human language? The modern Austrian philosopher Ludwig Wittgenstein captures this point perfectly: if human words are incapable of describing the aroma of coffee, how can they cope with something *really* complicated?

The basic idea which Aquinas develops is enormously important, and remains of permanent significance in Christian thought. It is usually referred to as 'the principle of analogy'. God reveals himself in forms which relate to our everyday experience. On account of the frailty and limitations of our human intellects, God reveals himself in ways that we can understand. He accommodates himself to our capacity (to use a favourite phrase of John Calvin, to which we shall return later).

Let's look at an illustration to make this point. Consider the statement 'God is our Father'. Aquinas argues that this means that God is *like* a human father. In other words, God is analogous to a father. In some ways he is like a human father, and in others he is not. There are genuine points of similarity. God cares for us, as human fathers care for their children (note Mt. 7:9–11). God is the ultimate source of our existence, just as our fathers brought us into being. He exercises authority over us, as do human fathers. Equally, there are genuine points of dissimilarity. God is not a human being, for example! Nor does the necessity of a human mother point to the need for a divine mother.

The point that Aquinas is trying to make is clear. God reveals himself in images and ideas which tie in with our world of everyday existence – yet which do not reduce God to that everyday world. When we say that 'God is our father', we don't mean that he is just yet another human father. Rather, we mean that thinking about human fathers helps us think about God. They are analogies. Like all analogies, they break down at points. However, they are still extremely useful and vivid ways of thinking about God.

Why is the use of analogy so important? Two points can be made. First, analogies point to God's ability to reveal himself in ways which we can understand. The scriptural images of God (for example, as shepherd, king, and father) are deceptively simple. They are easy to visualize and remember, yet on further reflection, they convey important and profound truths concerning God. The doctrine of the incarnation points to God's willingness and ability to come down to our level. God reveals himself in ways appropriate to our level and our abilities as human beings, using illustrations which we can handle.

It is easy to think about God as a shepherd, or a father. Yet this doesn't mean that God *is* a shepherd, or that God *is* a human father. That would be to reduce God to a purely human level. Rather, they tell us that shepherds and human fathers help us think about what God is like. God is *like* a shepherd or a human father. These images are not *identical* with God, yet are *analogous* with him. Analogies mean that God is revealed in our terms, without being reduced to our level.

A further illustration may make this clearer. Scripture often compares God to a rock (*e.g.*, Pss. 18:2; 28:1; 42:9; 78:35; 89:26). Yet this doesn't mean that God *is* a rock! That would be to make God into a physical object, opening the way for all sorts of idolatrous ideas. In reality, of course, what is being said is something rather different. Nobody is saying that God really is an inanimate natural object such as a rock. God is *like* a rock, in that he is stable, strong and supportive.

Second, analogies are memorable. They are powerful visual images, which stimulate our imagination. They get us thinking about God. Talking about God in abstract terms can get very boring and unimaginative. We all know that a picture is worth a thousand words. It is correct to talk about God as one who cares for us, guides us, and accompanies us throughout life. But it is much more memorable to talk about God as a shepherd – an analogy which makes all those points. People can remember the idea of God as a shepherd, linking it with key scriptural passages (like Ps. 23). And as they think about those images, they can begin to unpack the various ideas which they convey.

The parables which Jesus himself told are perhaps classic illustrations of this point. These parables are vivid images of everyday life, which act as windows through which we can catch a glimpse of God. Complicated ideas – such as forgiveness, or the coexistence of good and evil in the world – are presented in simple pictures. The parables in no way reduce God to the level of the natural world. They demonstrate God's ability and determination to reveal himself in ways which we can remember and understand. It's a concession to our human frailty and weakness, which God knows and understands. Paul also uses examples from everyday life to make important theological points (*e.g.*, Gal. 3:15).

But, as we all know from experience, analogies break down. There comes a point when they cannot be pressed further. How do we know when they break down? Let's look at an example, before moving on to consider its solution. The New Testament talks about Jesus giving his life as a 'ransom' for sinners (Mk. 10:45; 1 Tim. 2:6). What does this analogy mean? The everyday use of the word 'ransom' suggests three ideas.

1. *Liberation.* A ransom is something which achieves freedom for a person who is held in captivity. When someone is kidnapped, and a ransom demanded, the payment of that ransom leads to liberation.
2. *Payment.* A ransom is a sum of money which is paid in order to achieve an individual's liberation.
3. *Someone to whom the ransom is paid.* A ransom is usually paid to an individual's captor, or his agent.

These three ideas thus seem to be implied by speaking of Jesus' death as a 'ransom' for sinners.

But are they *all* present in Scripture? There is no doubt whatsoever that the New Testament proclaims that we have been liberated from captivity through the death and resurrection of Jesus. We have been set free from captivity to sin and the fear of death (Rom. 8:21; Heb. 2:15). It is also clear that the New Testament understands the death of Jesus as the price which had to be paid to achieve our liberation (1 Cor. 6:20; 7:23). Our liberation is a costly and a precious matter. In these two respects, the scriptural use of 'redemption' corresponds to the everyday use of the word. But what of the third aspect?

There is not a hint in the New Testament that Jesus' death was the price paid to someone (such as the devil) to achieve our liberation. Some of the writers of the first four centuries, however, assumed that they could press this analogy to its limits, and declared that God had delivered us from the power of the devil by offering him Jesus as the price of our liberation. This idea, however, is without scriptural warrant, and actually amounts to a serious distortion of the New Testament understanding of the meaning of the death of Jesus Christ. It is therefore important to consider how far we are allowed to press analogies before they break down, and mislead us.

Scripture does not give us one single analogy for God or for salvation, but uses a range of analogies. Each of these analogies illuminates certain aspects of our understanding of God, or the nature of salvation. However, these analogies also interact with each other. They modify each other. They help us understand the limits of other analogies. No analogy or parable is exhaustive in itself; taken together, however, the range of analogies and parables builds up to give a comprehensive and consistent understanding of God and salvation.

An example of how images interact may make this point clearer. Take the analogies of king, father and shepherd. Each of these three analogies conveys the idea of authority, suggesting that this is of fundamental importance to our understanding of God. Kings, however, often behave in arbitrary ways, and not always in the best interests of their subjects! The analogy of God as a king might thus be misunderstood to suggest that God is some sort of tyrant. However, the tender compassion of a father towards his children commended by Scripture (Ps. 103:13–18), and the total dedication of a good shepherd to the welfare of his flock (Jn. 10:11), show that this is not the intended meaning! Authority is to be exercised tenderly and wisely.

Of course, the analogy works the other way as well.

Earthly rulers, fathers and pastors are meant to model their conduct after the likeness of God, who sets them an example of how they should behave. Rulers should be persons of total integrity and dedication, committed to the well-being of their people. Fathers should exercise authority over their children with kindness and compassion. Pastors should demonstrate tenderness and dedication towards those commited to their care. Analogies thus help us think about God, and also about the way in which God would like his world to be.

This two-way relationship between human analogy and divine reality avoids an important difficulty. Many people find the idea of God as father unhelpful, on account of their negative experience of their own fathers. 'If God is like my father, I don't want anything to do with him.' Some human fathers are simply tyrants; the image of God this suggests is thoroughly unattractive. It is also totally unacceptable. Certain human fathers are found wanting in the light of what Scripture suggests that fatherhood should imply. Scripture commends certain patterns of fatherhood, in the first place as models for human fathers to imitate, and in the second, to govern our thinking about God himself. While all fathers may mirror God to some extent, some reflect God considerably better than others. Anyone who finds the idea of God as father difficult, on the basis of his or her experiences of human fathers, will find it helpful to reflect on this point.

Aquinas' doctrine of analogy, then, is of fundamental importance to the way we think about God. It illuminates the manner in which God reveals himself to us through Scripture. It helps us understand how God can be *above* our world, and yet simultaneously reveal himself *in* that world. God is not an object or a person in space and time; nevertheless, such persons and objects can help us deepen our appreciation of who God is, and what he is like. God, who is infinite, is able to express himself in human words and finite images. Yet, as Aquinas stressed, no contradiction is involved: God is able to reveal himself reliably and adequately in human words and images.

For Further Reading

Colin Brown, *Philosophy and the Christian Faith*, pp. 20–32. A useful introduction to and summary of the arguments for the existence of God discussed in this chapter.

F. C. Coplestone, *Aquinas*. Probably the best introduction available to the life, times and ideas of Aquinas.

Alister McGrath, *Understanding Jesus*, pp. 123–36. A discussion of the main scriptural analogies of salvation.

Alister McGrath, *Understanding the Trinity*, pp. 45–77. A detailed discussion of the idea of 'analogy', with special reference to analogies of God.

Erik Persson, *Sacra Doctrina*. A detailed study of the relation between reason and revelation according to Aquinas. Difficult reading, but recommended for the enthusiast.

Keith E. Yandell, *Christianity and Philosophy*, pp. 48–97. A more detailed analysis of the arguments for the existence of God discussed in this chapter.

CHAPTER FIVE

MARTIN LUTHER:

I: Faith and Experience

HANS Luder was an impoverished miner from the small town of Eisleben, in north-eastern Germany. His family were of peasant stock, as was that of his wife, Margarethe. In 1484, the Luder family moved to the neighbouring town of Mansfeld, where Hans was eventually able to buy his way into the copper-smelting industry. By 1491, he had become established as one of the leading citizens of the town. Hans Luder had made good.

Late in the evening of 10 November 1483, the Luders' first son was born. On the following morning, he was baptized. There was an ancient tradition that children were named after the saint upon whose day they were baptized. November 11 was the feast of St Martin of Tours, one of the patron saints of France. The boy was accordingly named Martin.

Martin was proud of his humble origins, even in a period which despised peasants. 'I am the son of a peasant,' he later wrote. 'My father, my grandfather and my great grandfather were all true peasants.' His schooling was modest, but good enough to allow him to go up to the University of Erfurt in April 1501. In January 1505 he gained his master's degree, and was ready to begin the study of that most lucrative of all medieval professions – the law. On 20 May of that same year, he began to immerse himself in the study of the law.

There were three options open to gifted students at medieval universities. After gaining their master's degree, they could proceed to one of the three 'higher faculties' –

theology, medicine or law. Like John Calvin, Martin chose to study law. Hans was fully behind his son's decision. In fact, he probably brought considerable pressure on his son to choose this career. Even before Martin turned to study law, his father had already bought a set of legal textbooks to allow him to get ahead. It would ensure future prosperity and status for his son. Hans began to look around for a wealthy bride to help Martin get on in the world.

Then Martin's career took an abrupt new turn. At some point around 30 June 1505, he was returning to Erfurt from a visit to Mansfeld. As he neared the village of Storterheim, a severe thunderstorm gathered around him. Suddenly, a bolt of lightening struck the ground next to him, throwing him off his horse. Martin was terrified. In his terror, he cried out, 'St Anne, help me! I will become a monk!' St Anne was the patron saint of miners, which perhaps allows us to understand why Martin called upon her.

Martin's friends tried to make him forget about that vow. Nevertheless, he decided to stand by it. On 17 July 1505, he entered one of the seven major monasteries at Erfurt. He chose the most rigorous of them all – the Augustinian monastery. His father was outraged at the decision, and remained alienated from his son for some considerable time.

Nevertheless, Martin persevered. His new vocation allowed him to begin the serious study of theology. The Erfurt Augustinian monastery had close links with the university, with several of its leading personalities being members of the faculty of theology. He was able to wrestle with the great names of late medieval religious thought – William of Ockham, Pierre d'Ailly, and Gabriel Biel. Above all, however, he was able to begin the detailed study of Scripture. Martin was given a copy of the Vulgate, the standard medieval Latin translation of Scripture.

His career developed well. After two years in the monastery, he was ordained priest in 1507. By 1509, he had gained his first major theological qualification. Finally, on 18 October 1512, he was awarded the degree of Doctor of Divinity, the culmination of his academic studies. By then, however, he had moved from Erfurt, and established himself at the nearby town of Wittenberg.

The University of Wittenberg was founded in 1502 by Frederick the Wise. His motives in establishing this seat of learning were not entirely educational: he wanted to overshadow the reputation of the neighbouring university of Leipzig. However, Frederick's dream came to nothing. Within a decade, Wittenberg had established a well-deserved reputation for mediocrity. Student numbers were dangerously low. Martin took up a chair of biblical studies at Wittenberg immediately after gaining his doctorate, and remained there (apart from occasional periods of absence) for the rest of his life.

In the years which followed, he lectured upon the Psalms (1513–1515), and the letters to the Romans (1515–1516), Galatians (1516–1517) and Hebrews (1517–1518). In the course of lecturing on these biblical works, he found his understanding of the way in which God deals with his world changing. His theology was forged through continual wrestling with the scriptural text. As he meditated upon Scripture, Martin found himself becoming increasingly critical of some of the doctrines and practices of the late medieval church. He also began to read Augustine, especially the anti-Pelagian writings, in some detail. Gradually, he came to develop a reforming theology which would have momentous consequences for the history of Europe and the Christian church.

The first rumbling came in 1517, with the controversy over indulgences. The sixteenth century was an age which knew how to enjoy its sins, and the possibility of being able to sin without undue anxiety concerning the consequences was enormously attractive. Indulgences seemed to offer just this possibility. For the payment of a sum of money, indulgence-sellers such as Johann Tetzel seemed to offer forgiveness of sins – past, present and future – with the full authority of the pope. This authority was not limited to the living either. Tetzel assured his hearers that their dead relatives could be released from any punishment due for their sins. He even had an advertising jingle to promote his indulgence trafficking:

> As soon as the coin in the coffer rings,
> The soul from purgatory springs!

For Martin, this was a total perversion of the gospel. It made nonsense of the New Testament. It turned Christianity into a marketable commodity, aimed at those who wanted to indulge themselves in sin. So he protested. On 31 October 1517, he nailed his celebrated Ninety-Five Theses on the main door of the Castle Church at Wittenberg. The importance of this event must not be over-estimated. All that Martin was really doing was posting a legitimate university notice on the university's main notice-board. He was calling a public university debate on the theology of indulgences, as he was entitled to. However, some printers got hold of copies of Martin's text, and realized its commercial possibilities. Within months, the Ninety-Five Theses were circulating widely, and Martin was being talked of as an angry young man. This reputation was confirmed in 1519, when he met Johann Eck in public disputation at Leipzig and challenged the authority of the pope.

Martin lived in a world in which the humanist movement was gaining an increasingly wide hearing. Although the word 'humanist' nowadays suggests atheism or secularism, in the sixteenth century it had none of these overtones. It meant 'someone who places great emphasis upon the sources of classical antiquity'. One of the conceits of the age was to invent Latin or Greek versions of names, in order to lend them a little more dignity. Thus Philip Schwarzerd called himself 'Melanchthon' (literally, 'black earth'), and Johann Hauschein adopted the name 'Oecolampadius' (literally, 'house light'). At some point around 1519, Martin Luder himself fell victim to this trend of the age.

By then, Martin was gaining a reputation as a critic of the medieval church. His emphasis upon Christian freedom – brilliantly expressed in the 1520 writing *On the Freedom of a Christian* – led him to play around with his surname, 'Luder'. He altered this to 'Eleutherius' – literally, 'liberator'. Within what seems to have been a very short period of time, Martin tired of this pretension. But the new way of writing his family name remained. Martin Luder had become Martin Luther.

In 1520, Luther published three major works which immediately established his reputation as a major popular reformer. Shrewdly, Luther wrote in German, making his ideas accessible to a wide public: Latin was the language of the intellectual and ecclesiastical elite of Europe, whereas German was the language of the common people. In the *Appeal to the Christian Nobility of the German Nation*, Luther argued passionately for the need for reform of the church. In both its doctrine and its practices, the church of the early sixteenth century had cast itself adrift from the New Testament. His pithy and witty German gave added popular appeal to some intensely serious theological ideas.

Encouraged by the remarkable success of this work, Luther followed it up with *The Babylonian Captivity of the Christian Church*. In this powerful piece of writing, Luther argued that the gospel had become captive to the institutional church. The medieval church, he argued, had imprisoned the gospel in a complex system of priests and sacraments. The church had become the master of the gospel, where it should be its servant. This point was further developed in *The Liberty of a Christian*, in which Luther stressed both the freedom and obligations of the believer.

By now, Luther was in trouble. On 15 June 1520, Luther was censured by a papal bull, and ordered to retract his views. He refused, adding insult to injury by publicly burning the bull. He was excommunicated in January of the following year, and summoned to appear before the Diet of Worms. Again, he refused to withdraw his views. Luther's position became increasingly serious. Realizing this, a friendly German prince arranged for him to be 'kidnapped', and took him off to the safety of the Wartburg, a castle near Eisenach. During his eight months of isolation, Luther had time to think through the implications of many of his ideas, and to test the genuineness of his motives. By the time he returned to Wittenberg in 1522 to take charge of the Reformation in that town, his ideas were gaining considerable support throughout Europe. The Reformation had begun.

Even as a young man, Luther was intensely aware of his own sinfulness and weakness. How could a sinner such as himself ever enter into fellowship with a holy and righteous God? How could someone such as himself ever come to trust and love a God who punished sinners? Anxiety over this question led Luther to plunge himself deep into the study of Scripture. Eventually he emerged in possession of the doctrine of justification by faith. How Luther came to discover this doctrine and what it implies will be discussed in the chapter which follows. In the remainder of the present chapter, we are concerned with one of Luther's most important contributions to Christian thought: his 'theology of the cross', which illuminates the relation between faith and reason, and provides helpful insights into suffering.

In the years 1518–1520, Luther felt increasingly under threat from the ecclesiastical and political powers of his day. It seemed to him, as it seemed to many other observers of his situation, that his days were numbered. Suffering and death seemed to draw near to him. But what meaning should suffering and death have for the Christian? Luther seems to have pondered this difficult question at some length in these years of growing crisis. The outcome of his reflections is what is now generally known as the 'theology of the cross (*theologia crucis*)'.

For Luther, the cross is the centre of the Christian faith. The haunting image of the crucified Christ is the crucible in which all our thinking about God is forged. Luther expresses the centrality of the cross in a series of terse statements, such as 'The cross alone is our theology', and 'The cross puts everything to the test'. Luther draws a now-famous distinction between the 'theologian of glory', who seeks God apart from Jesus Christ, and the 'theologian of the cross', who knows that God is revealed in and through the cross of Christ.

But what sort of revelation might this be? In what way is God revealed in the cross? Luther develops the idea of a *hidden revelation* of God in the cross. This is a difficult idea.

However, once grasped, it is remarkably helpful in making sense of many aspects of Christian existence and experience. Perhaps the best way to understand what Luther means by a 'hidden revelation' is to consider the scene of helplessness and hopelessness on that first Good Friday, as Jesus Christ died upon the cross.

The crowd gathering round the cross were expecting something dramatic to happen. If Jesus really was the Son of God, they could expect God to intervene and rescue him. Yet, as that long day wore on, there was no sign of a dramatic divine intervention. In his cry from the cross, even Jesus himself experienced a momentary yet profound sense of the absence of God, 'My God, my God, why have you forsaken me?' Many expected God to intervene dramatically in the situation, to deliver the dying Jesus. But nothing of the kind happened. Jesus suffered, and finally died. There was no sign of God acting in that situation. So those who based their thinking about God solely on experience drew the obvious conclusion: God was not there.

The resurrection overturned that judgment. God was revealed as having been present and active at Calvary, working out the salvation of humanity and the vindication of Jesus Christ. He was not *perceived* to be present – but present he really was. What experience interpreted as the *absence* of God, the resurrection showed up as the *hidden presence* of God. God may have been experienced as inactive, yet the resurrection showed God to have been active behind the scenes, working in secret. For Luther, the resurrection demonstrates how unreliable the verdict of human experience really is. Instead of relying upon the misleading impressions of human experience, we should trust in God's promises. God promises to be present with us, even in life's darkest hours – and if experience cannot detect him as being present, then that verdict of experience must be considered unreliable.

Luther suggests that we think of human existence as being like that first Good Friday. We see many things which puzzle and frighten us, and lead us to conclude that God is absent from or inactive in that situation. Suffering is an excellent example. How, we often wonder, can God be present in human suffering? Much the same thoughts must have passed through the minds of those watching Jesus Christ suffer and die. The first Easter Day, however, transformed that situation, and our understanding of the way in which God is present and active in his world. It showed that God is present and active in situations in which experience thinks he is absent and inactive – such as suffering.

According to Luther, we should apply this insight to our own situation. There are times when all of us find it difficult to accept that God is present and active – suffering being a case in point. If we try to think of these times in the light of Good Friday, we can see that those same thoughts and fears were expressed then. Yet the resurrection overturned those thoughts and fears, showing us how unreliable human experience is in these matters. We could summarize these insights like this:

CROSS-EXPERIENCE	RESURRECTION-FAITH
God is absent	God is present in a hidden manner
God is inactive	God is active in a hidden manner
Misplaced trust in reason	Proper trust in the promises of God
Suffering is meaningless	God works out salvation through suffering

Our present experience seems like Good Friday. God may not seem to be obviously present and active. But just as faith sees Good Friday from the standpoint of Easter Day, so it must also see the same patterns of interpretation in present experience. What *looks like* divine absence is really hidden divine presence.

This has important results for Luther's understanding of faith. Faith is an ability to see God's presence and activity in the world, and in our own experience. Faith sees behind external appearances and the misleading impressions of experience. It is an openness, a willingness, to find God where he has promised to be, even when experience suggests that he is not there. Luther uses the phrase 'the darkness of faith' to make this point. This has important

64

results for Luther's understanding of the nature of doubt.

Doubt shows up our natural tendency to base our judgments upon experience, rather than faith. When faith and experience seem to be out of step with each other, we tend to trust our experience, rather than faith. But, Luther points out, how unreliable a guide experience turns out to be. Those who trusted in experience on the first Good Friday looked very foolish in the light of the resurrection. For Luther, the resurrection demonstrates the superiority of faith in the promises of God over reliance upon experience or reason. We must learn to let God be God, and trust in him and his promises, rather than in our own finite and inadequate perception of a situation.

The cross thus destroys our confidence in our own ability to discern what God is like. It shatters our misplaced trust in reason and experience to let us know who God is, and what he is like. It forces us to admit defeat, to concede our need to be told about God, instead of deciding in advance what he is like. By revealing himself through the suffering, weakness and shame of the cross, God forces us to abandon our preconceived ideas about him. God breaks down our preconceptions about him, so that we will be more willing to learn from him. Humility is essential, if we are to encounter and deepen our knowledge of the God who was present and active at Calvary.

Finally, Luther insists that there is one experience which is basic to being a theologian. He describes this briefly in one of his most quoted (and most difficult) statements. 'It is living, dying, and even being condemned which makes a theologian – not reading, speculating and understanding.' When I first read these words of Luther, I found them baffling. Surely theology was about reading Scripture, and trying to make sense of it? What was Luther complaining about? Now I know, and I am convinced that Luther is right. To be a *real* theologian is to wrestle with none other than the living God – not with ideas about God, but with God himself. And how can a sinner ever hope to deal adequately with this God?

If you want to be a real theologian, Luther insists, you must have experienced a sense of condemnation. You must have had a moment of insight, in which you realize just how sinful you really are, and how much you merit the condemnation of God. Christ's death on the cross spells out the full extent of God's wrath against sin, and shows us up as ones who are condemned. It is only from this point that we can fully appreciate the central theme of the New Testament – how God was able to deliver sinners from their fate. Without a full awareness of our sin, and the dreadful gulf this opens up between ourselves and God, we cannot appreciate the joy and wonder of the proclamation of forgiveness through Jesus Christ.

Just about anyone can read the New Testament, and make some sort of sense of it. But, Luther insists, the *real* theologian is someone who has experienced a sense of condemnation on account of sin – who reads the New Testament, and realizes that the message of forgiveness is good news for him or her. The gospel is thus experienced as something liberating, something which transforms our situation, something which is relevant to us. It is very easy to read the New Testament as if it were nothing more than any other piece of literature. And Luther reminds us that it is only through being aware of our sin, and all its implications, that we can fully appreciate the wonder of the electrifying declaration that God has forgiven our sins through Jesus Christ.

Luther's account of the relation between faith and experience is one of the most interesting and difficult aspects of his thought. It is remarkably helpful in beginning to think through questions such as the nature of doubt, and the way in which we detect God's presence and activity in the world, and in our own personal lives. Luther, however, is best known for his doctrine of justification by faith alone. What this doctrine is, and why it is so important, will be dealt with in the following chapter.

For Further Reading

Probably the best biography of Luther is Roland Bainton, *Here I Stand*, strongly recommended as the most readable introduction currently available.

A excellent more recent biography is James M. Kittelson, *Luther the Reformer*.

For a general introduction to the intellectual and social background to the Reformation, see Alister McGrath, *Reformation Thought*, pp. 1–66.

For more detailed studies of his career and ideas, see: Bernhard Lohse, *Martin Luther: An Introduction*; Walther von Loewenich, *Martin Luther: The Man and His Work*; Alister McGrath, *Luther's Theology of the Cross*; and Gordon Rupp, *The Righteousness of God*.

For reflections on the unreliability of experience in relation to the Christian life, see Alister McGrath, *Doubt*, pp. 133–9.

For detailed exposition of the modern theological relevance of the 'theology of the cross', see: Alister McGrath, *The Enigma of the Cross* and Jürgen Moltmann, *The Crucified God*.

CHAPTER SIX

MARTIN LUTHER:

II: The Justification of the Sinner

BY all accounts, the young Luther was intensely aware of his own sinfulness. One question seemed to have dominated his early life. 'How can I find a gracious God?' How can a righteous God ever enter into a relationship with a sinner? Aware of his sin, Luther found such questions deeply depressing. Every time he thought about Jesus Christ, he found himself picturing Christ as a stern judge, exposing and condemning his sin.

Central to Luther's difficulties was the idea of the 'righteousness of God'. What did it mean to say that God was righteous? As a student of theology, Luther had been trained according to a school of thought sometimes known as 'Nominalism', although it is now more usually known as 'the Modern Way'. Important writers belonging to this group included the great fourteenth-century English writer William of Ockham (best known for 'Ockham's Razor'), and the fifteenth-century German writer Gabriel Biel. As a young man, Luther became familiar with their writings and ideas, including their distinctive ideas concerning what it meant to say that God was 'righteous'.

Let's outline the views of Gabriel Biel, to get an idea of what Luther would have thought about the 'righteousness of God' in his early years. According to Biel, God had entered into a contract or covenant with humanity. If human beings did certain definite things (such as loving God and ceasing to sin), God would respond by justifying them. God was scrupulously impartial: it wasn't *who* you were that counted, but *what* you did. Anyone who met the basic precondition laid down by the covenant would be justified, irrespective of who he or she was. It didn't matter whether you were a king or a peasant – the same precondition applied. God was righteous, in that he rewarded anyone who fulfilled the precondition for justification, and punished anyone who didn't.

But what, Luther wondered, if you were a sinner? What happened if you were so trapped by sin that you couldn't meet the basic precondition? Luther appears to have recognized that sin exercised a deep hold over his life, so deep that he couldn't turn his back on it. It was all very well to promise him justification if he stopped sinning – but that was like promising a blind man a million dollars, provided he could see! It just wasn't possible to meet the precondition. It seemed to Luther that Biel's views on justification and the 'righteousness of God' were quite unrealistic, and failed to take human sin seriously. If God, in his righteousness, punished sinners, then the gospel held no comfort for sinners such as Luther.

Luther relates how he tried with all his power to do what was necessary to achieve salvation, but found himself more and more convinced that he could not be saved.

> I was a good monk, and kept my order so strictly that I could say that if ever a monk could get to heaven through monastic discipline, I was that monk. All my companions in the monastery would confirm this . . . And yet my conscience would not give me certainty, but I always doubted and said, 'You didn't do that right. You weren't contrite enough. You left that out of your confession.' The more I tried to remedy an uncertain, weak and troubled conscience with human traditions, the more I daily found it more uncertain, weaker and more troubled.

It seemed to Luther that he simply could not meet the preconditions of salvation. He did not have the resources needed to be saved. There was no way that God could justly reward him with salvation – only condemnation.

So at some point in the period 1513–1514, Luther found his attention centring on one passage of Scripture: 'in the gospel a righteousness of God is revealed' (Rom. 1:17). Luther could not see how the revelation of the 'righteousness of God' was gospel, 'good news'. If God was righteous, he would punish sinners – such as Luther! What was good news about that? Why should Paul get so excited about something so negative? Or had he, Luther, misunderstood Paul altogether?

And then at some point – probably in 1515, but we are not sure exactly when – Luther seems to have had a breakthrough. Fortunately, we have his own account of what happened. In the final year of his life (1545), Luther published a brief account of his theological reflections as a young man, in which he relates how he found himself deeply troubled by Romans 1:17. Luther recalls that he was taught to interpret the 'righteousness of God' as that righteousness by which God himself is righteous and punishes sinners, so that (as far as he could see) the revelation of the 'righteousness of God' in the gospel was nothing other than the revelation of the wrath of God directed against sinners. How could this be good news for *sinners*? Luther continues:

> At last, by the mercy of God, meditating day and night, I gave heed to the context of the words, namely 'In it the righteousness of God is revealed', as it is written, 'He who through faith is righteous shall live'. There I began to understand that the righteousness of God is that by which the righteous lives by a gift of God, namely by faith. And this is the meaning: the righteousness of God is revealed by the gospel, namely the passive righteousness with which merciful God justifies us by faith, as it is written, 'He who through faith is righteous shall live'. Here I felt that I was altogether born again and had entered paradise through open gates.

This passage vibrates with the excitement of discovery, as Luther relates how he came to realize that the righteousness of God which is revealed in the gospel is *a gift of God given to sinners*. The God who is revealed in the gospel is not a harsh judge, who judges us on the basis of our merits, but a merciful and gracious God who gives his children something which they could never attain by their own unaided efforts.

In other words, the 'righteousness of God' is not the righteousness which *belongs to* God, but that which *comes from* God. Gabriel Biel had interpreted it as God's own personal righteousness, the righteousness which belonged to God, and on the basis of which he judges us; Luther now realized that it meant the righteousness which God gives to us, as a gift. God himself meets the precondition for justification! Instead of sinners having to become righteous before they can enter into fellowship with God, God himself gives them that righteousness, so that they can stand before him.

An illustration may help make Luther's new approach clearer. Let us suppose that you are in prison, and are offered your freedom on condition that you pay a heavy fine. The promise is real – so long as you can meet the precondition, the promise will be fulfilled. Gabriel Biel (and Pelagius before him) work on the presupposition, initially shared by Luther, that you have the necessary money stacked away somewhere. As your freedom is worth far more, you are being offered a bargain. So you pay the fine. This presents no difficulties – so long as you have the necessary financial resources! Luther increasingly came to share the view of Augustine – that sinful humanity just doesn't have the resources needed to meet this precondition. To go back to our analogy, Luther (and Augustine before him) work on the assumption that, as you don't have the money, the promise of freedom has little relevance to your situation. For both Augustine and Luther, therefore, the good news of the gospel is that you have been *given* the necessary money with which to buy your freedom. In other words, the precondition has been met for you by someone else. What you don't have has been provided by someone else – unexpectedly and undeservedly. Now Luther could see why Paul was so excited about the revelation of the righteousness of God in the gospel (Romans 1:17)!

What, then, did Luther come to understand by the 'righteousness of God'? In a series of images, Luther builds up a picture of a righteousness given to us by God, which remains outside us. Just as a mother hen covers her chicks with her wing, so God clothes us with his righteousness. Although we are unrighteous in ourselves, God endows us with his protective and healing righteousness, beneath which we may begin to grow in holiness. It is something which shields us. It is something which is given to us, something which we ourselves could never obtain by our own efforts. We stand as justified sinners before God, clothed with a righteousness which is not our own, but is given to us by God himself. Our righteous standing with God, the fact that we are 'right with God' through the faith which he gives us, is ultimately due to the overwhelming grace of God, rather than our efforts to make ourselves righteous in his sight. The great theme of 'justification by faith alone' – so characteristic of Luther – extols the graciousness and generosity of God as much as it affirms the impotence of sinful humanity to justify itself. Even the faith through which we are justified is a gift of God!

Luther thus argues that we are righteous on account of God having clothed us with his righteousness – but inside, we are still sinners. God justifies us on the basis of his gift of righteousness, rather than on the basis of any righteousness which we may possess. This idea underlies one of Luther's most characteristic phrases, in which he refers to sinners as being 'righteous and sinners at one and the same time (*simul iustus et peccator*)'. Although we are sinners, God is still able to renew and regenerate our fallen natures. Just as workmen on a building site may cover their work with tarpaulins to protect it from the weather, so God protects his work of renewal and regeneration within us with the external covering of his righteousness.

A distinction is made between God's work outside us and inside us. Externally, God imputes, or reckons, to us the righteousness of Christ, which alters our status; internally, he works to renew our fallen and sinful natures, which changes our being. God's action outside us takes the form of an event, while his work within us takes the form of a process. Later Protestant writers would refer to the work of God outside us as 'justification', and the work of God within us as 'sanctification'; Luther, however, does not make this distinction at this stage.

Although we remain sinners, we thus live in hope, knowing that God is at work within us, renewing and rebuilding us. Luther argues that justified sinners are like people who are ill, yet who have been entrusted to the care of a competent physician. They are righteous 'not in fact, but in hope (*non in re sed in spe*)'. The signs of recovery and regeneration within us point to our future perfection in righteousness, just as a patient under the care of a good physician can rest assured of being cured as he detects signs of recovery.

What does the phrase 'justification by faith' mean? The idea of 'justification', which is frequently employed by Paul (*e.g.*, Rom. 5:1), refers to the restoration or establishment of a relationship between a sinner and God, taking in ideas such as 'forgiveness' and 'reconciliation'. But what does 'justification *by faith*' mean? Luther emphasizes that it does *not* mean that we are justified on account of faith! It doesn't mean that the sinner is justified because he or she believes, on account of that faith. That would amount to making faith a human work, something which we do or achieve. Rather, it means that we receive everything necessary for justification – including faith – from God.

The doctrine of justification by faith alone is an affirmation that God does everything necessary for salvation. Even faith itself is a gift from God. God is active, and we are passive; God graciously gives, and we joyfully receive. We are not justified on the basis of our own merit, actions or moral virtue, but on the basis of a divine gift to us. Luther stresses that we do not become righteous by doing good deeds, but that we do good deeds because we are righteous. In other words, good works are a response to God having given us his righteousness as a gift; it isn't as if God gives us his righteousness on condition that we start doing good deeds. Righteous living is the *result*, not the *precondition*, of justification.

This view was regarded by many of Luther's critics as outrageous. It seemed to suggest that God had no time for good works. Luther was branded as a libertine and as an 'antinomian' – in other words, someone who has no place for the law (Greek: *nomos*) in the religious life. Perhaps we could use the word 'anarchist' to convey much the same idea. In fact, Luther was simply stating that good works are not the *cause* of justification, but are its *result*. In other words, Luther treats good works as the *natural result of having been justified*, rather than the *cause of that justification*. Far from destroying morality, Luther simply saw himself as setting it in its proper context. Believers perform good works as an act of thankfulness to God for having forgiven them, rather than in an attempt to get God to forgive them in the first place. The Swiss reformer Heinrich Bullinger made much the same point in 1554, when he published a work on this subject with the comprehensive, if not particularly eloquent, title: *The grace of God that justifies us for the sake of Christ through faith alone, without good works, while faith meanwhile abounds in good works.*

Luther further develops his understanding of the 'righteousness of God' in terms of a 'wonderful exchange' between Christ and the believer. Using the analogy of a human marriage, Luther argues that Christ and the believer are united through faith: Christ bestows his righteousness upon the believer, and the believer's sin is transferred to Christ. Justification involves no legal fiction, but the real personal union of the risen Christ and the individual believer. Everything that is Christ's becomes ours, and all that is ours becomes his. Luther thus speaks of 'a grasping faith (*fides apprehensiva*)' which grabs hold of Christ, and unites him to the believer, in order that this wonderful exchange of attributes may take place. Luther insists that justification involves a change in an individual's status before God, rather than a fundamental change in his nature: although the individual believer is righteous by faith, he remains a sinner. The presence of sin within the believer thus in no way contradicts the fact that he or she has been justified.

It will be clear that Luther's doctrine of justification by

faith has considerable implications for individual believers. Their salvation rests upon a work of God, not any work of theirs. It is something which they receive as a gift, rather than something which they have to earn as a reward. In many ways, this is a very radical idea. Outside the Christian churches today, salvation is widely regarded as something which could be earned or merited through good works. People often suggest that they 'aren't good enough to be Christians'. Luther would agree! It is not because we are good that God justifies us; we are good because God justifies us. For Luther, the recognition that we are sinful and totally unworthy of the grace of God is the first step in receiving that grace, as a totally unmerited and transforming gift.

Important though the doctrine of justification by faith is for individuals, it also had considerable social implications at the time of the Reformation. This can be seen from the Indulgence Controversy of 1517, which first brought Luther to prominence. What was an indulgence? Originally, an indulgence seems to have been a gift of money to charity as an expression of thankfulness for forgiveness. By the beginning of the sixteenth century, however, this innocent idea had been transformed into an important source of income for the papacy. Luther's wrath was particularly kindled by the marketing techniques of the authorized indulgence seller, Johannes Tetzel. For a mere three marks, a sinner could be released from all punishments he would otherwise have faced in purgatory – and many found this an offer difficult to refuse at the price! Perhaps more sinister was Tetzel's suggestion that it would be possible to release the soul of a loved one from its sufferings in purgatory. For Luther, this suggested that God's forgiveness could be purchased or earned – a suggestion which seemed totally inconsistent with the New Testament emphasis upon the grace of God. It was his outrage at this suggestion which led to his posting the celebrated Ninety-Five Theses on indulgences on the door of the Castle Church at Wittenberg on 31 October 1517.

Yet the idea that you could purchase forgiveness was actually quite widespread at the time. Many people genuinely believed that the eternal penalties resulting from sinful actions could be reduced, if not eliminated, by a cash payment. Thus Cardinal Albrecht of Brandenburg managed to accumulate a remission of purgatorial penalties reckoned to total 39,245,120 years. In the early sixteenth century indulgences were a major source of papal revenue – and, as the somewhat dubious deal between the pope, Albrecht of Brandenburg and the banking house of Fuggers indicates, that income found its way into a number of coffers. As a result, there were a number of vested interests concerned to ensure that the early sixteenth-century vagueness concerning the doctrine of justification was maintained.

Luther's doctrine of justification by faith, with its associated doctrine of the 'priesthood of all believers', thus assumed an importance which went far beyond the sphere of academic theology. It cut the ground from under vested church interests. Forgiveness was a matter between the believer and God: no others were involved. No priest was required to pronounce that he had been forgiven – the believer could read in Scripture the promises of forgiveness to those who confessed their sins, and needed no-one to repeat them or execute them. No payment of any kind was required to receive divine forgiveness. The concept of purgatory, upon which so much popular superstition and ecclesiastical exploitation was based, was dismissed as a non-scriptural fiction. With the rejection of the existence of purgatory went a whole attitude to death and dying, and the practices previously associated with them. The new emphasis, derived partly from Renaissance individualism and partly from the New Testament, upon the individual's relation with God effectively marginalized the role of the institution of the church. It was not merely income from indulgences which Luther attacked – it was also the view of the role of the church in forgiveness which lay behind this practice.

Luther's action in posting the Ninety-Five Theses on indulgences on 31 October 1517 (now celebrated as 'Reformation Day' in Germany) was not merely a protest against Tetzel's indulgence advertisements, which rivalled those of modern detergent manufacturers in terms of their optimistic claims. Nor was it merely a request that the church might clarify its teaching on forgiveness. It marked the appearance of a new theology of forgiveness (or, more accurately, the *re*appearance of an old and apparently forgotten theology of forgiveness) which threatened to remove from the institutional church any role in forgiveness – thus threatening the vested interests of the pope, many clergy, some princes and one rather important banking house. The doctrine of justification by faith alone reaffirmed that God's forgiveness was given, not bought, and was available to any, irrespective of their financial means or social condition. The related doctrine of the 'priesthood of all believers' meant that the believer, with the gracious assistance of God, could do everything necessary to his or her own salvation without needing to involve either priest or church. It is thus little wonder that Luther's views were regarded with such anxiety by the ecclesiastical establishment, and received with great interest by so many laity at the time!

But what is the importance of Luther's doctrine of justification in our own day and age? Modern western society, especially in the United States of America, is very achievement-orientated. Many of us find it difficult to accept that God loves us because of the values instilled into us by our families and peers. For example, we might be perfectionists, who feel that we must *do* something or *achieve* something before God can love us. If we are this sort of person, the gospel proclamation of the *unconditionality* of God's love for us can be difficult to accept – it contradicts the standards of western culture. Or we may have been taught that dependency is to be discouraged. Some individuals believe strongly in the cult of independence: personal fulfilment is based on not being dependent on anyone or anything. The idea that God loves us is an invitation to learn to depend on God. This clashes with the set of values we have been taught by our peers, who believe that the way to get ahead in the world is through being independent.

Luther's doctrine of justification by faith mounts a

powerful challenge to these attitudes. Our status before God is something given, not something earned. As Luther himself put this: 'Sinners are attractive because they are loved; they are not loved because they are attractive.' God's love for us is not dependent upon our achievements, nor can we ever earn our salvation. We do not need to be high achievers to become Christians; it is God, not us, who achieves things! The tranquility of faith – so powerful a theme of Luther's spirituality – rests upon recognizing that God has done all that is necessary for our salvation in Jesus Christ, and has done it well.

For Further Reading

Most of the items listed under the previous chapter are also of relevance here. They may be supplemented with the following suggestions.

For an introduction to the importance of the doctrine of justification at the time of the Reformation, with particular reference to Luther, see Alister McGrath, *Justification by Faith*, pp. 47–62.

For a detailed analysis of the development of Luther's breakthrough, see Alister McGrath, *Luther's Theology of the Cross*.

CHAPTER SEVEN

HULDRYCH ZWINGLI:
Remembering Jesus

MOST people think of the Reformation as something that happened in Germany, mainly under the influence of Martin Luther. However, the movement also developed in Switzerland, apparently quite independently of Luther to start with. At the same time as Luther was defending his ideas at the Leipzig Disputation (1519), Zwingli was beginning his programme of reform at Zurich. The importance that historians and theologians attach to Luther often results in the Swiss Reformation being overlooked, and its chief reformer being eclipsed.

At that time, Switzerland was much smaller than it is at present. The name 'Switzerland' is based on one of the three original cantons – Schwyz, Uri and Unterwalden – who signed a treaty of mutual defence against the Austrians in 1291. This confederation was gradually enlarged. In 1332, Lucerne joined the confederation, followed by Zurich (1351), Glarus and Zug (1352), and Berne (1353). The strength of this confederation was demonstrated at the battle of Näfels (1388), at which an historic victory ensured its survival. In 1481, the cantons of Solothurn and Fribourg joined the confederation, bringing the total membership to ten. In 1501, Basel and Schaffhausen joined, followed by Appenzell in 1513. No further cantons joined the confederation until the aftermath of the French Revolution.

Zwingli was born on New Year's Day, 1484 in the Toggenburg valley in the canton of St Gallen, in the eastern part of modern-day Switzerland. Strictly speaking, St

Gallen was not part of the Swiss confederation. However, in the treaty of 1451, St Gallen had allied itself to some of the Swiss cantons, and Zwingli always appears to have regarded himself as Swiss.

After an initial period of education at Berne, Zwingli attended the University of Vienna (1498–1502). Vienna was widely regarded as one of the most exciting universities close to Switzerland, on account of the university reforms then taking place. Under the guidance of leading humanists, such as Conrad Celtis, the university was adopting humanist reforms. He then moved to the University of Basel (1502–6), where he strengthened his humanist position. In 1506, he was ordained priest, and served in this capacity at Glarus for the next ten years, before moving to serve at a shrine at Einsiedeln in 1516.

Everything that we know about Zwingli in this early period points to his being strongly influenced by humanism. As we have already seen (pp. 60–61), to twentieth-century readers, 'humanist' means something like 'secular' or 'atheist'. But this wasn't what the word 'humanism' meant at the time of the Renaissance or Reformation. Humanism was about developing written and spoken eloquence, using the Latin and Greek classics as a model. It meant going back to the great literary works of antiquity, and reading them in their original languages. A humanist was basically someone who placed emphasis on the importance of speaking and writing well, and who felt that these skills were best developed by studying the classics. The slogan 'back to the sources (*ad fontes*)' neatly summarizes this approach.

The relevance of humanism to Christianity will be obvious. In the first place, humanism wasn't anti-Christian or non-Christian. It was about going back to key original sources. For literary purposes, these sources were the Latin and Greek classics; for religious purposes, it was the New Testament. The best theology is to be done by going back to Scripture, and reading it in its original languages. Instead of poring over medieval works of scholastic theology, readers should proceed directly to Scripture, and meditate on what they find there. In many ways, the rise of humanism may be seen as setting the scene for the Reformation. Two factors help explain why this is the case.

First, there was a new emphasis on the study of Scripture itself. In other words, theologians were pointed towards Scripture as the most important resource available for the study and understanding of Christianity. All other sources were, at best, of secondary importance. This general principle passed into the thought of the Reformation as the 'Scripture principle'. If something couldn't be directly demonstrated from Scripture, it wasn't necessary for faith. That didn't mean it was wrong – just that you couldn't tell anyone that they *ought* to believe it. For example, most of the reformers (including Luther and Calvin) were happy to keep the practice of infant baptism, even though it isn't directly mentioned in Scripture, because they felt that it could be justified on the basis of Scripture. On the other hand, they rejected the practice of praying for the dead, which they felt could not be justified in this way.

Second, Scripture was to be studied in its original languages, not in Latin translation. As we noted earlier (p. 58), the most commonly used form of the Bible available in the Middle Ages was known as the Vulgate. This was a Latin translation of the Bible, including both the Old and New Testaments, and also those books now generally referred to as the Apocrypha or 'deuterocanonical works'. But it wasn't a very good translation; some of its vocabulary led the medieval church astray. Some illustrations will indicate the kind of problems that arose.

What did Jesus say when he began his ministry in Galilee? According to the Vulgate, Jesus spoke the following words: '*Do penance*, for the Kingdom of God is at hand'. This would seem to refer to the church rite of penance. But, armed with the best Greek scholarship, humanists such as Lorenzo Valla and Erasmus of Rotterdam pointed out that the correct translation was rather different: '*Repent*, for the Kingdom of God is at hand' (Mt. 4:17). The reference is clearly to a change of mind, or a change of heart, on the part of the hearer of the message – not to a church service!

What did Gabriel say to Mary, on telling her that she was

81

to bear Jesus? According to the Vulgate, the angel's words were: 'Greetings, *you that are full of grace.*' This would seem to imply that Mary is like a reservoir, full of grace, which individuals can draw on in time of need. And so a whole theology came to be based upon this verse, seeing in Mary a source of God's grace. But, as the humanist translators pointed out, the Greek could not bear this meaning, and ought to be translated, 'Greetings, *you that are highly favoured*' (Lk. 1:28). In other words, Mary had found favour in the sight of God, as a result of which she was to bear the saviour of the world. There is no hint of the 'reservoir of grace' idea. So another major theme of medieval theology was shown to rest on quite inadequate scriptural foundations.

The return to studying Scripture in its original languages thus placed question marks against some traditional teachings of the medieval church. These often seemed to rest on faulty translations of biblical passages. This was an important weapon in the armoury of the Reformers, who wanted to bring both the teachings and the practices of the church back to those found in Scripture.

Third, Scripture was made much more widely available. Before the invention of printing in the fifteenth century, works were produced in manuscript. This was a tedious and expensive process, by which works had to be copied by hand. It was virtually impossible for a lay person to get hold of a copy of the Bible. The invention of printing, however, meant that books could be produced cheaply and in large numbers. It became increasingly common for printed New Testaments to be found on the bookshelves of lay persons in the early sixteenth century. The Bible became accessible, allowing a much greater readership to reflect on whether the church was faithful to its foundations in Scripture.

The humanist contribution to this publishing boom was of major importance. Humanist scholars, such as Erasmus of Rotterdam, produced printed editions of the New Testament in its original Greek, and also Greek and Hebrew grammars to enable scholars to make sense of what they read. As a result, more and more people were able to read and understand Scripture in its original languages. An educated laity arose, who felt capable of making sense of Scripture for themselves. The clerical monopoly on reading and understanding Scripture had come to an end.

Zwingli was a typical biblical humanist, able to read and understand the New Testament in its original Greek. Fascinated by its ideas, he became acutely aware of the obvious differences between the New Testament church and the catholic church of the later Middle Ages. Zwingli was particularly concerned with the obvious differences in morals and structures that he saw. As a result, he thought of a programme of reform in terms of reforming the life and morals of the church, on the basis of the New Testament model. Whereas Luther placed emphasis on reforming the *doctrine* of the church, Zwingli was initially more concerned with reforming the *life* of the church and individual Christian believers.

In 1518 Zwingli received an invitation which was to change his own life, and also that of the church in western Europe. He was invited to take up a pastoral post at the Great Minster (*Grossmünster*) in Zurich. This was by far the largest church building in Zurich, and carried with it considerable prestige. By then, Zurich had established itself as a leading city in the Swiss Confederation. By any standards, this was an important post. On Saturday 1 January 1519 – the day of his thirty-fifth birthday – Zwingli began his ministry at Zurich.

It became obvious immediately that Zwingli was a reformer. The day after his arrival, he announced his intention of beginning a new course of sermons. He proposed to deliver a continuous course of sermons on the gospel according to Matthew. Instead of relying on commentaries, he would base his sermons directly on the scriptural text. For Zwingli, Scripture was a living and liberating text. It was the means by which God was able to speak to his people, and allow them to break free from bondage to false ideas and practices. Before long, controversy gathered, as Zwingli spoke out against false understandings of the gospel.

The City Council grew anxious at the unrest which was growing within the city, and decided to settle the matter. In January 1523, a great public disputation was arranged between Zwingli and his catholic opponents. The City Council sat in judgment, as Zwingli debated his programme of reform with some local catholic clergy. It soon became clear that Zwingli was gaining the upper hand. Able to translate without difficulty from Hebrew, Greek or Latin into the Zurich dialect, Zwingli displayed a mastery of Scripture which his opponents could not match. There could only be one outcome. The City Council decided that a programme of reform based on Scripture, such as that outlined by Zwingli, would become official city policy.

Encouraged by this success, Zwingli persuaded other city councils to have public debates along the same lines. A major breakthrough took place in 1528, when the city of Berne decided to adopt the Reformation after a similar public disputation. Berne was a major centre of political and military power in the region. Its political and military support for beleagured Geneva in 1536 would prove to be decisive in establishing Calvin's influence over the second phase of the Reformation. Calvin's success as a reformer owes more to Zwingli than is generally realized. Zwingli himself died in 1531, defending his Reformation on the field of battle.

Of Zwingli's many contributions to Christian thought, perhaps the most interesting is his explanation of why Christians celebrate the death of Jesus Christ in the service which is variously known as the Lord's Supper, Holy Communion, or the Eucharist. In the gospel accounts of the Last Supper (Mt. 26:17–29; Mk. 14:12–25; Lk. 22:7–20; note also 1 Cor. 11:23–5), we hear Jesus telling his disciples to 'do this' (that is, break and eat bread, and drink wine) 'in remembrance of me' (Lk. 22:19). But how does this help us to remember Jesus? And, perhaps more importantly, how are we to interpret Jesus' words, spoken at the time of breaking the bread: 'this is my body, given for you' (Luke 22:19). How can bread 'be' the body of Jesus? Zwingli's answers to both these questions are important and helpful. We begin by considering how

84

celebrating the Holy Communion enables us to remember Jesus.

Zwingli uses two helpful analogies to explain the link between the communion service and the death of Jesus. The first concerns a merchant, who has to leave home on a long and potentially hazardous business trip. Before he sets out, he leaves his wife his ring. While he is away, the ring will remind her of him. Although he is absent, the ring will recall his memory until he returns. The ring has strong links and associations with the merchant. Zwingli thus argues that the communion service recalls the memory of Jesus, and reminds us of his promise to return (note how well Paul's remarks at 1 Corinthians 11:23–5 fit in with this approach).

A second analogy draws on ideas of particular importance to Swiss national identity. Earlier, we noted how the great battle of Näfels (1388) was of central importance in ensuring the survival of the Swiss confederation. At that battle, the Swiss confederate forces defeated an Austrian army which threatened the independence of the confederation. The Swiss armies were drawn from various cantons: to show that they were on the same side, they wore a common emblem – a white cross, sewn on the shoulders of their clothing. This emblem identified the wearer as someone who had sworn allegiance to the Swiss confederation. It was a mark of identity and solidarity. (This same white cross is now the central symbol of the Swiss national flag).

So important was this victory that it was commemorated by an annual pilgrimage in Zwingli's time. On the first Thursday in April, it was the custom for individuals from the various cantons to make the journey to Näfels in the canton of Glarus, and give thanks for the victory gained there and pray for the continuing well-being of the Swiss confederation. The battle was treated as a foundational event of the Swiss confederation, a turning point in its history.

Zwingli uses these aspects of the battle of Näfels to explain the link between the communion service and the death of Jesus on the cross.

If a man sews on a white cross, he proclaims that he wishes to be a confederate. And if he makes the pilgrimage to Näfels and gives God praise and thanksgiving for the victory vouchsafed to our fore-fathers, he testifies that he is a confederate indeed. Similarly, the man who receives the mark of baptism is the one who is resolved to hear what God says to him, to learn the divine precepts, and to live his life in accordance with them. And the man who in the remembrance or supper gives thanks to God in the congregation testifies to the fact that from the very heart he rejoices in the death of Christ, and thanks him for it.

Sacraments (such as baptism or the communion) are thus public demonstrations of the allegiance of the believer to the Christian community. Just as the Swiss soldier at Näfels publicly proclaimed his loyalty to the Swiss confederation by wearing a white cross, so Christians proclaim their loyalty to the Christian community by remembering the death of Jesus through baptism and the communion. And just as the pilgrimage to Näfels recalled the memory of the great event on which the present existence of the Swiss confederation depended, so the communion service recalls the memory of the death and passion of Jesus, on which the present existence of the Christian community depends. The communion service reminds Christians that victory was gained through the death of Jesus.

For Zwingli, Christ's death has the same significance for the church as the battle of Näfels had for the Swiss con-federation. It is the foundational event of the Christian church, central to its identity and self-understanding. Just as the commemoration of Näfels does not involve the re-enactment of that battle, so the eucharist involves neither the repetition of the sacrifice of Christ, nor his presence at the commemoration. The eucharist is 'a mem-orial of the suffering of Christ'. It is as if Christ had said: 'I entrust to you a symbol of this my surrender and testa-ment, to awaken in you the remembrance of me and of my goodness to you, so that when you see this bread and this cup, held forth in this memorial supper, you may remember me as delivered up for you, just as if you saw me before you as you see me now, eating with you.'

So how are we to understand the words 'this is my body'? One theory, which became of especial importance during the Middle Ages, was known as transubstantiation. This Latin term literally means 'a change in substance'. According to this theory, the outward appearance of the bread remains unchanged. Its shape, taste, smell and colour all remain the same. But through some deep and mysterious process, the inner being of that bread is changed. It becomes the body of Christ. Aristotle referred to the outward appearances of things as 'accidents', and the inward reality as the 'substance'. According to the doctrine of transubstantiation, the accidents of the bread remain unchanged, while its substance changes from that of bread to that of the body of Jesus Christ.

Zwingli thought this theory was absurd. When Jesus said 'this is my body', the word 'is' didn't mean 'is *literally identical to*'. Zwingli illustrated this point by considering a related statement in the gospel of John: 'I am the bread of life' (Jn. 6:35). When Jesus said these words, Zwingli pointed out, he had not changed into a loaf of bread! The words are being used metaphorically. In other words, 'this is my body' doesn't mean 'this bread *is literally identical with* the body of Jesus Christ'; it means 'this bread *signifies* the body of Christ'. It reminds us of the breaking of the body of Jesus on the cross.

So in what way does the bread signify the body of Jesus? How can something so humble as a piece of bread ever represent something as important and as moving as the death of Jesus? Surely it isn't capable of this! Zwingli uses a number of analogies to show how this can, in fact, happen with perfect ease. Two of these are particularly helpful.

Take a king's signet ring, Zwingli suggests. Considered as a piece of metal, it isn't especially significant. It may even be made of gold – but it's still a *small* piece of gold. Yet the ring signifies the power and the authority of the king. It represents something much greater. When a small piece of gold is taken and made into the king's signet ring, it takes on a much deeper significance. What was once just a small piece of metal now comes to represent the full authority and majesty of the king. It signifies the king himself. In much the same way, Zwingli argues, the bread comes to bear a new significance. It comes to represent the precious death of the saviour of the world. Although it remains a piece of bread, it comes to have a new meaning and new associations – very precious associations.

Or again, Zwingli suggests, consider a lily. That lily can be picked, and made into a bridal crown. Although it remains a lily, it then comes to symbolize the happiness and mutual commitment of a marriage. It comes to have associations which it wouldn't have if it were just left growing in a field, or if it were plucked and placed in a vase. Its new context gives it a whole new significance. So it is with the bread, which is given a new context in the communion service, and hence a new meaning. It never stops being bread, just as the lily never stops being a lily. But it has new overtones and associations that weren't originally there.

A more modern illustration may make this point more clearly. Suppose you often have occasion to walk past a jeweller's shop. In the window is a display of rings. As you pass, you sometimes pause to admire them. As you pass by one day, you notice an assistant taking a ring from the window display, and handing it to a young man, who places it on the finger of a woman accompanying him. They have just become engaged, and the ring represents and symbolizes their commitment to each other. It is the same ring which was once in the window display, and is now on the woman's finger; it has not altered. But it has come to represent something different. It has come to have associations and a significance which go far beyond those it possessed earlier. The ring has a new context, and as a result a new meaning. It has become special, not because of what it is in itself, but on account of its associations.

The bread, then, becomes special on account of its powerful associations. It evokes the memory of the suffering and death of Jesus Christ. It acts as a catalyst for our thoughts, as we reflect on how costly a thing our redemption is. The image of the dying Christ, whose body was broken for us, becomes associated with the bread. And so it is that the bread stimulates and focuses our reflections, enabling us all to remember Jesus and all that he means for us and to us.

For Further Reading

The best biography of Zwingli currently available is G. R. Potter, *Zwingli*.

For a detailed examination of Zwingli's ideas, see W. P. Stephens, *The Theology of Huldrych Zwingli*.

For further information on the nature of humanism, and its impact on the Reformation, see Alister McGrath, *Reformation Thought*, pp. 27–49.

On the impact of humanism upon the study and interpretation of Scripture at the time of the Reformation, see Alister McGrath, *Reformation Thought*, pp. 95–116.

For further information on Zwingli's views on the sacraments, see Stephens, *The Theology of Huldrych Zwingli*, pp. 180–259; McGrath, *Reformation Thought*, pp. 117–30.

CHAPTER EIGHT

JOHN CALVIN:

Our Knowledge of God

THE first phase of the Reformation was dominated by a few charismatic individuals of considerable talent — men such as Luther at Wittenberg and Zwingli at Geneva. It soon became evident, however, that Luther's successors were men of relatively modest talents. They lacked the charisma and the vision of Luther. It also became obvious that both Luther and Zwingli had not developed an organized body of systematic teachings, on the basis of which their reforming work could be consolidated. The second generation of the Reformation needed, above all, someone who was an organizer, able to communicate the principles of the Reformation efficiently and effectively. A new star had to arise in the firmament of the Reformation, if the movement was to survive.

That star arose in the person of John Calvin. So successful was Calvin as an organizer, a teacher and a communicator that he has been compared to Lenin in the modern period — someone who was able to turn ideas into a revolution. By the time of his death, Calvin had virtually eclipsed his fellow reformers, and bequeathed a rich heritage to western Christianity. A new impulse and vitality was injected into the Reformation movement, which enabled it to break down national and cultural barriers in Europe and North America, doing much to shape the religious map of the modern world. Calvin was a man of ideas, rather than of action, and his ideas continue to provide much food for thought in our own day and age.

For many people, the name of Calvin is virtually

synonymous with that of Geneva. Although Geneva is now part of Switzerland, in the sixteenth century it was a small independent city state. Calvin, however, was a Frenchman. He was born on 10 July 1509 in the cathedral city of Noyon, about seventy miles north-east of Paris. His father was involved in the financial administration of the local diocese, and could rely on the patronage of the bishop to ensure support for his son. At some point in the early 1520s (probably 1523), the young Calvin was sent up to the University of Paris.

After a thorough grounding in Latin grammar at the hands of Mathurin Cordier, Calvin entered the Collège de Montaigu. After completing his rigorous education in the arts, Calvin moved to Orléans to study civil law, probably at some point in 1528. Although Calvin's father had originally intended that his son should study theology, he appears to have changed his mind. His father seems to have realized that the study of law, Calvin later remarked, generally makes people rich. It is also possible that Calvin's father may have lost the patronage of the local bishop on account of a financial wrangle back at Noyon.

It is generally thought that Calvin's detailed study of civil law gave him access to methods and ideas which he would later exploit in his career as a reformer. It was at Orléans that he learned Greek. At some point in 1529 Calvin moved to Bourges, attracted by the fame of the great Italian lawyer Andrea Alciati. Most Calvin scholars consider that Calvin's great clarity of expression is due to the influence of Alciati.

Soon after graduating in law, Calvin had to return to Noyon. His father was ill, and died in May 1531. He had been excommunicated by the local cathedral chapter. Freed from family obligations (his mother died while he was a child), Calvin returned to Paris to continue his studies, and became increasingly sympathetic to the reforming ideas then gaining an excited hearing in that city. The university and city authorities, however, were intensely hostile to Luther's ideas. On 2 November 1533, Calvin was obliged to leave Paris suddenly. The rector of the University of Paris, Nicolas Cop, had delivered a university address in which he openly supported Luther's doctrine of justification by faith. The Parliament at Paris immediately took action against Cop. A copy of Cop's address exists in Calvin's handwriting, suggesting that he may have composed the address. At any rate, Calvin fled Paris, fearful for his safety.

By 1534 Calvin had become an enthusiastic supporter of the principles of the Reformation. During the following year, he settled down in the Swiss city of Basle, safe from any French threat. Making the best use of his enforced leisure, he published a book destined to exercise a decisive effect upon the Reformation: the *Institutes of the Christian Religion*. First published in May 1536, this work was a systematic and lucid exposition of the main points of the Christian faith. It attracted considerable attention to its author, who revised and expanded the work considerably during the remainder of his life. The first edition of the book had six chapters; the final edition, published in 1559 (and translated by Calvin into his native French in 1560), had eighty. It is generally regarded as one of the greatest works to emerge from the Reformation.

After winding up his affairs in Noyon early in 1536, Calvin decided to settle down to a life of private study in the great city of Strasbourg. Unfortunately, the direct route from Noyon to Strasbourg was impassable, due to the outbreak of war between Francis I of France and the Emperor Charles V. Calvin had to make an extended detour, passing through the city of Geneva which had recently gained its independence from the neighbouring territory of Savoy. Geneva was then in a state of confusion, having just evicted its local bishop and begun a controversial programme of reform under the Frenchmen Guillaume Farel and Pierre Viret. On hearing that Calvin was in the city, they demanded that he stay, and help the cause of the Reformation. They needed a good teacher. Calvin reluctantly agreed.

His attempts to provide the Genevan church with a solid basis of doctrine and discipline met intense resistance. Having just thrown out their local bishop, the last thing that many Genevans wanted was the imposition of new religious obligations. Calvin's attempts to reform the doctrine and discipline of the Genevan church were fiercely resisted by a well-organized opposition. After a series of quarrels, matters reached a head on Easter Day 1538: Calvin was expelled from the city, and sought refuge in Strasbourg.

Having arrived in Strasbourg two years later than he had anticipated, Calvin began to make up for lost time. In quick succession he produced a series of major theological works. He revised and expanded his *Institutes* (1539), and produced the first French translation of this work (1541); he produced a brilliant defence of Reformation principles in his famous *Reply to Sadoleto* (Sadoleto had written to the Genevans, inviting them to return to the Roman Catholic church); and his skills as a biblical exegete were demonstrated in his *Commentary on the Epistle to the Romans*. As pastor to the French-speaking congregation in the city, Calvin was able to gain experience of the practical problems facing reformed pastors. Through his friendship with Martin Bucer, the Strasbourg reformer, Calvin was able to develop his thinking on the relation between the city and church.

In September 1541, Calvin was asked to return to Geneva. In his absence, the religious and political situation had deteriorated. The city appealed to him to return, and restore order and confidence within the city. The Calvin who returned to Geneva was a wiser and more experienced young man, far better equipped for the massive tasks awaiting him than he had been three years earlier. Although Calvin would still find himself quarrelling with the city authorities for more than a decade, it was from a position of strength. Finally, opposition to his programme of reform died out. For the last decade of his life, he had virtually a free hand in the religious affairs of the city. At the time of his death in 1564, Calvin had made Geneva the centre of an international movement, which came to bear his name. Calvinism is still one of the most potent and significant intellectual movements in human history.

In turning to deal with Calvin's religious thought, we are confronted with an embarrassment of riches. Calvin's writings, especially the 1559 edition of the *Institutes*, are both brilliant and lucid, combining considerable intellectual depth and originality with a remarkable ability to communicate. Virtually any aspect of Calvin's thought is worth studying. The particular theme we have chosen is of major importance to many Christians. How do we know God? How can human language ever do justice to God? How can the richness and profundity of God ever be expressed in the words of human beings? How can the gulf between God and human beings be bridged?

Calvin begins by asking how we know anything about God. To make his points, he enters into a dialogue with Cicero's classical treatise *On the nature of the gods*. Cicero suggests that human beings have a natural knowledge of the existence of higher beings, such as gods. Human beings, by reflecting on nature, are able to arrive at a belief in the existence of gods. Calvin develops this view, relating it to Paul's assertion of a natural knowledge of God (Rom. 1:19–20). 'There is, within the human mind, by natural instinct, an awareness of divinity ... To prevent anyone from taking refuge in the pretence of ignorance, God himself has implanted in all human beings a certain understanding of his divine majesty.' Anyone who contemplates nature is aware of a sense of the presence of God.

Anyone who has walked at night under a star-studded sky, with tiny points of light suspended in the blackness of space, will appreciate the point that Calvin is making. At times, the presence, power and majesty of a creator God seem to be written into the fabric of his creation. It is almost as if God, like a master artist, signed his name upon his creation for all to see. But how far does this deep sense of the presence of God take us?

Calvin argues that humans can arrive at a knowledge of God's existence (and also his nature) from intelligent use of reason. He makes two fundamental criticisms of this knowledge, however. In the first place, it is *fragmentary*; in the second, it is *inconsistent*. A knowledge of God arrived at by reason can only allow us very limited access to God. There is every danger, Calvin argues, that we will fail to appreciate the definite limits placed upon our abilities to

94

reason, on account of our human finiteness. Furthermore, nature is ambiguous, some of its aspects pointing to the existence of God, and others suggesting his absence. This means that ideas of God (or the gods) arrived at through purely human reason will be inconsistent and unreliable. On the basis of reason alone, human beings will not be able to reach agreement on what God is like.

By reflecting on nature, reason may indeed be able to tell us that God is a creator, and that he is wise and eternal. But we need access to more detailed knowledge of God than this! We need to know how he may be encountered. We need to know how to live our lives in accordance with his purposes. And where is that knowledge to be found?

Calvin argues that such knowledge is to be found in Scripture. Scripture *confirms* and *extends* a natural human knowledge of God. It confirms the basic human instinct that there is a creator of this world, and that this creator is wise and eternal. It is consistent with what we already know. But it goes further than this. It tells us that we are sinners, and how God is working out our salvation through Jesus Christ. It explains to us what we must do if we are to be saved, and what the Christian life is like.

By allowing a natural knowledge of God, Calvin lays the foundations for his theory of revelation. In his revelation of himself through Scripture and in Jesus Christ, God confirms the limited insights of nature and reason, and takes these still further. Nature and reason are like a point of contact for revelation. Any religion or philosophy which is based solely on nature or reason will be uncertain, fragmentary and inadequate. But God builds upon natural insights, which ultimately derive from his having created both the natural order and humanity itself. In that God stamped his presence upon creation, and created human beings in his image and likeness (Gn. 1:26–7), it is not unreasonable that we should be able to discern God's presence in nature.

Christianity, Calvin declares, insists that natural insights about God are genuine, but inadequate. They are like a road which leads only part of the way to a destination: they point in the right direction, but don't take us all the way

there. They need supplementation. And God, in his provi-
dence and mercy, has provided just such a supplement in
Scripture. Scripture confirms the basic human instinct that
God *is* there, and tells us more about who he is, what he is
like, and what he intends for us. 'Nearly all the wisdom we
possess,' Calvin writes, 'that is to say, true and sound wisdom, consists of two parts: the knowledge of God and of
ourselves.' Scripture provides both parts of this knowledge, and shows how they are related. We can only understand ourselves, our nature and our destiny, when we have
'first looked upon the face of God'. Scripture allows us to
look upon the face of God, especially as revealed in the
person of Jesus Christ.

Having argued for the reasonableness and necessity of
divine revelation, Calvin begins to explore the particular
form it takes. In Scripture, God reveals himself verbally, in
the form of words. But how can words ever do justice to
the majesty of God? How can words span the enormous
gulf between God and sinful humanity. Calvin's discussion
of this question is generally regarded as one of his most
valuable contributions to Christian thought. The idea
which he develops is usually referred to as the 'principle of
accommodation'. The word 'accommodation' here means
'adjusting or adapting to meet the needs of the situation'.

In revelation, Calvin argues, God adjusts himself to the
capacities of the human mind and heart. God paints a
portrait of himself which we are capable of understanding.
The analogy which lies behind Calvin's thinking at this
point is that of a human orator. A good speaker knows the
limitations of his audience, and adjusts the way he speaks
accordingly. The gulf between the speaker and the hearer
must be bridged if communication is to take place. The
limitations of his audience determine the language and
imagery the orator employs. The parables of Jesus illustrate this point perfectly: they use language and illustrations (such as analogies based on sheep and shepherds)
perfectly suited to his audience in rural Palestine. Paul also
uses ideas adapted to the situation of his hearers, drawn
from the commercial and legal world of the cities in which
the majority of his readers lived.

In the classical period orators were highly educated and verbally skilled, whereas their audiences were generally unlearned and lacked any real ability to handle words skilfully. As a result, the orator had to come down to their level if he was to communicate with them. He had to bridge the gap between himself and his audience by understanding their difficulties in comprehending his language, imagery and ideas. Similarly, Calvin argues, God has to come down to our level if he is to reveal himself to us. God scales himself down to meet our abilities. Just as a human mother stoops down to reach her child, so God stoops down to come to our level. Revelation is an act of divine condescension, by which God bridges the gulf between himself and his capacities, and sinful humanity and its much weaker abilities. Like any good speaker, God knows his audience – and adjusts his language accordingly.

The same idea may be found in earlier writers. For example Origen (a third-century Greek Christian writer well versed in the skills and techniques of rhetoric) often suggests that God faced the same problems in addressing sinful humanity as those experienced by a human father in trying to communicate to small children. 'God condescends and lowers himself, accommodating himself to our weakness, like a schoolmaster talking a "little language" to his children, like a father caring for his own children and adopting their ways.' When you are talking to small children, you have to appreciate that they have limited intellectual resources at their disposal. If you treat them as adults, and use words and ideas that are beyond their understanding and experience, you will fail to communicate with them. You have to adapt yourself to their capacities. We can paraphrase Origen's discussion of this point, as found in his *Homilies on Jeremiah*, as follows:

When God involves himself in human affairs, he adapts himself to human ways of speaking and thinking. When we talk to a child of two years age, we talk baby-talk because he is a child. If we behaved and spoke to that child in a way suitable for adults, and did not adapt ourselves to his situation, he would be totally unable to understand us. Now imagine a similar situation confronting God when he comes to deal with the human race, and especially those who are still babies. After all, human beings often use different words for things when speaking to children than those they use when speaking to other adults. Yet this does not point to intellectual immaturity on their part! When dealing with children, for the sake of accommodation, we speak the language of children, rather than the language of older and mature people.

An example of this accommodation is provided by the scriptural portraits of God. God, Calvin points out, is often represented as if he has a mouth, eyes, hands and feet. That would seem to suggest that God is a human being. It might seem to imply that somehow the eternal and spiritual God has been reduced to a physical human being, like us! (The question at issue is often referred to as 'anthropomorphism' – in other words, being portrayed in human form.) Calvin argues that God is obliged to reveal himself in this pictorial manner on account of our weak intellects. God has to adjust the way in which he speaks of himself to take into account our strictly limited ability to comprehend him. Images of God which represent him as having a mouth or hands are divine 'baby-talk', a way in which God comes down to our level and uses images which we can handle. More sophisticated ways of speaking about God are certainly proper – but we might not be able to understand them.

Calvin uses three main images to develop this idea of divine accommodation to human capacities in revelation. God is our *father*, who is prepared to use the language of children in order to communicate with us. He adapts himself to the weakness and inexperience of childhood. He is our *teacher*, who is aware of the need to come down to our level if he is to educate us concerning himself. He adapts himself to our ignorance, in order to teach us. He is our *judge*, who persuades us of our sinfulness, rebelliousness and disobedience. Just as human rhetoric in a court of law is designed to secure a verdict, so God is concerned to convince and convict us of our sin; to let *his* verdict become *our* verdict, as we realize that we are indeed sinners, who are far from God. Calvin insists that true wisdom lies in the knowledge of God and of ourselves: it is through recognizing that we are sinners that we discover that God is our redeemer.

The doctrine of the incarnation speaks of God coming down to our level to meet us. He comes among us as one of us. Calvin extends this principle to the language and images of revelation: God reveals himself in words and pictures we can cope with. God is prepared to stoop down, as a mother stoops down to meet her child, and use language which we can understand. God's concern and purpose is to communicate, to bridge the great yawning gulf between himself as creator and humanity as his creation. For Calvin, God's willingness and ability to condescend, to scale himself down, to adapt himself to our abilities, is a mark of God's tender mercy towards us and care for us.

For Further Reading

An excellent and highly readable account of Calvin's career is to be found in T. H. L. Parker, *John Calvin*.

Useful biographical material, along with an exposition of the leading ideas of Calvin's thought, may be found in François Wendel, *Calvin*.

A careful study of Calvin's early period, with a detailed examination of the date and nature of his 'conversion', may be found in Alexandre Ganoczy, *The Young Calvin*.

The basic themes of this chapter may be studied in depth from two articles: F. L. Battles, 'God was Accommodating Himself to Human Capacity' and E. Grislis, 'Calvin's Use of Cicero in the Institutes'. These articles are well worth dipping into, although it is necessary to have access to a good theological library to obtain the journals in which they are published.

For the subsequent influence of Calvin on Europe and North America, see the collection of essays brought together in *International Calvinism* ed. Menna Prestwich.

Calvin's *Institutes of the Christian Religion* are worth dipping into. The 1559 edition has been well translated by F. L. Battles.

CHAPTER NINE

JONATHAN EDWARDS:

The Challenge of Modern Culture

THE Reformation marked a turning point for Christian theology. Luther, Zwingli and Calvin, along with a galaxy of minor stars, changed the face of the Christian church in Europe and laid the foundations of the later great expansion into North America. The insights of the Reformation movement were chiefly developed within Puritanism in England and colonial North America. The word 'Puritan' immediately conjures up images of ranting preachers whose chief interest in life was to prevent anyone having any fun. This is precisely the image of Puritanism that those hostile to the movement wanted to create. In reality, Puritanism was rather different. It was a movement with a passionate concern for spiritual renewal and growth, a genuine pastoral interest in the spiritual and physical well-being of the community, and a burning desire to defend and proclaim the truth and relevance of the Christian gospel to its own day and age. During the final part of the sixteenth century, and throughout the seventeenth, Puritanism was a major force throughout the world of English-speaking Christianity.

Although Puritanism had its origins in sixteenth-century England, its chief influence was to be found in seventeenth-century colonial North America, which became the home of many Calvinists in the seventeenth century. Seventeenth-century England was an intolerant society, especially during the reign of Charles I. In 1620 the Pilgrim Fathers sailed from Plymouth. Between 1627 and 1640 some 4,000 individuals made the hazardous crossing of the Atlantic Ocean, and settled on the coastline of Massachussets Bay. For them, America was the promised land, and they were the chosen people. Expelled from their Egypt by a cruel Pharoah, they had settled in a land flowing with milk and honey. They would build a new Jerusalem, a city upon a hill, in this strange land. They might be far from the country of their birth, but they were close to God.

By the end of the first quarter of the eighteenth century, however, it seemed to many that New England Puritanism had lost its way. It appeared to have run out of steam. Its days seemed to be numbered. Growing material prosperity brought with it an indifference to faith, which soon became reduced to morality. The future of Christianity in the New World seemed to be in doubt. A sense of listlessness, of despondency, appears in many Christian writings of the period. Older Christians began to become intensely nostalgic, longing for the old days of their youth. What would happen next?

The first clues began to be noticed in 1727. Theodore Freylinghausen, a Dutch pastor ministering to a congregation in the Raritan Valley of New Jersey, began to notice signs of a revival. Like a forest fire fanned by the wind, the revival began to spread, through the agency of individuals such as Gilbert Tennent. From New Jersey it found its way to Pennsylvania and Virginia. But it was in 1734 that the smouldering revival exploded into flame, to become what history now knows as 'the Great Awakening'. An extraordinary series of events took place in Northampton, Massachussets, in response to the preaching of the man now widely regarded as the greatest and most influential American theologian – Jonathan Edwards.

Edwards was born at East Windsor, Connecticut, on 5 October 1703. His father was a local pastor, under whose ministry a series of revivals would take place in the 1720s. In September 1716 Edwards entered Yale College, New Haven (now Yale University), where he later served as tutor from 1724 to 1726. When he was around seventeen years of age, Edwards underwent a conversion experience. As he read 1 Timothy 1:17, he was overwhelmed by a sense of God's greatness and glory. 'As I read the words,' he wrote later in his personal journal, 'there came into my soul, and it was, as it were, diffused through it, a sense of the glory of the divine Being; a new sense quite different from anything I ever experienced before.'

In 1726 Edwards resigned his post at Yale in order to take up a pastoral charge at Northampton, as the colleague of his maternal grandfather, Solomon Stoddard. Stoddard was widely regarded as the leading spiritual authority in the Connecticut Valley – so much so, in fact, that people were prone to call him 'Pope Stoddard' behind his back. Edwards was ordained on 15 February 1727, aged twenty-three. In July of the same year, he married Sarah Pierrepont, with whom he had been in love for some considerable time. His grandfather died in February 1729, leaving Edwards in charge of one of the most important churches in the area. Reflecting on the events of those two years, Edwards noted an absence of any general interest in religion: Northampton, like virtually all of colonial North America, 'seemed to be at that time very insensible of the things of religion, and engaged in other cares and pursuits.'

At that time, congregations and their pastors alike lacked spiritual vitality. In the early seventeenth century New England churches would only admit to full membership individuals who could testify to a personal experience of conversion. As the century progressed, fewer and fewer individuals could testify to such an experience. Yet most individuals wanted some kind of connection with the church – for example, to have their children baptized, or to have a Christian burial service. From about 1660 onwards, a 'half-way' membership was recognized: anyone who was prepared to accept the truth of Christianity and the moral discipline of the church could have his or her children baptized.

The result of this was inevitable: by the beginning of the eighteenth century a large proportion of church members were 'nominal' or 'half-way'. They might attend church, and learn from the preaching of the word of God; they might have their children baptized; they might recognize

Christianity as true and morally helpful – but they were, in the final resort, unconverted. Christianity and church membership were viewed as just another part of American society. Being baptized and attending church were just part and parcel of being a good citizen. The pastors of such congregations themselves often seemed to lack any personal faith. Although generally well-educated, they lacked any sense of the real relevance of the gospel. Increasingly, Christianity came to be viewed in purely moral and social terms. The English preacher George Whitefield, visiting North America, summarized the situation as follows: 'I am greatly persuaded that the generality of preachers talk of an unknown, unfelt Christ. And the reason why congregations have been so dead is because dead men preach to them.'

That situation changed at Northampton, radically and suddenly, in the winter of 1734–1735. The final weeks of 1734 witnessed several conversions, 'very remarkably and suddenly, one after another.' The revival continued into the new year, reaching its peak during the months of March and April 1735. There was hardly a household in the town that was not affected. Perhaps as many as three hundred individuals, 'about the same number of males as females', appeared to have been converted. The local tavern became deserted. Those who used to while away their spare time drinking turned to spending time with Edwards instead. Christianity, once something strange, distant and external, became something inward, vital and real.

> Persons after their conversion often speak of religious things as seeming new to them; that preaching is a new thing; that it seems to them that they never heard preaching before; that the Bible is a new book; they find there new chapters, new psalms, new histories, because they see them in a new light. Here was the remarkable instance of an aged woman, of above seventy years, who had spent most of her days under Mr Stoddard's powerful ministry. Reading in the New Testament concerning

Christ's suffering for sinners, she seemed aston-
ished at what she reads, at what was very real and
beautiful, but quite new to her. At first, before she
had time to turn her thoughts. she wondered within
herself, that she had never heard of it before; but
then immediately recollected herself, and thought
that she had often heard it, and read it, but never till
now saw it as real.

Throughout, the same theme recurs: Christianity became
real. What was known by the head became known by the
heart.

Edwards published accounts of the events at Northampton in the form of a book, *A Faithful Narrative of the Sur-
prising Work of God*, which drew international attention to
the awakening. Between 1737 and 1739 the book went
through three editions and twenty printings. As evangelical revival gathered momentum in North America and
England, the happenings at Northampton were seen as the
harbingers of that dawn.

As the revival continued in New England, it was given a
new sense of direction by George Whitefield, recently
arrived from England. Edwards found that he was no
longer at the forefront of the revival movement. He was
also troubled by divisions within his congregation at
Northampton, particularly over matters of church discipline. He moved to minister to a congregation at
Stockbridge, where relatively light parish duties allowed
him to write a series of major theological works which gave
intellectual muscle to New England Puritanism. American
Christianity had come of age. In 1757, his reputation as a
scholar firmly established, Edwards was invited to become
president of the College of New Jersey, Princeton (now
Princeton University). Following an unsuccessful inocul-
ation against small-pox, he died at Princeton on 22 March
1758.

Of Edwards' many contributions to Christian theology,
that singled out for discussion here concerns the challenge
posed to the proclamation of the gospel by the rise of
modern culture. The reason for focusing on this aspect of

Edwards' thought is that it is intensely relevant for anyone concerned with proclaiming the gospel in modern western culture. Eighteenth-century New England saw the birth of attitudes which are now commonplace among many westerners, especially in modern North America. In the 1730s Edwards wrestled with the problem posed by a cluster of attitudes which were beginning to become a serious obstacle to the preaching of the gospel. (He called these attitudes collectively 'Arminianism', although this term is not particularly helpful and need not concern us further.) These attitiudes are similar, in many ways, to Pelagianism (see chapter 2), but with features characteristic of the American scene. It might be more helpful to refer to this movement as 'achievement Christianity'. The passage of time has made this problem increasingly relevant, especially in cultures which are achievement and success-orientated. To illustrate the problem, we may consider two difficulties Edwards faced as he began his ministry at Northampton.

The first difficulty centred on the idea of the 'self-made person'. An emphasis upon personal achievement was evident in a number of areas of life. Commercial prosperity was held to be based upon personal dedication, worth and sheer hard work. 'You are what you achieve' seems to have been the motto of many individuals at Northampton, particularly those who would eventually succeed in having Edwards expelled from the town.

To individuals such as these, the leading Reformation idea of 'justification by faith apart from works' was at best silly, and at worst outrageous. It suggested that their personal achievements were of little consequence in getting right with God. In fact, it even seemed to imply that these achievements might get in the way of their coming to faith. Far more acceptable to such people was the idea that Christianity was basically some useful spiritual assistance and support in the quest for self-achievement. In other words, they wanted their religion to be about God respecting and endorsing their accomplishments.

A second difficulty arose from the 'half-way' covenant,

which encouraged congregations to admit nominal Christians. In his church, Edwards thus encountered a large number of individuals who had been baptized for the sake of social convention, and who viewed attending church as a civil duty. The idea that they were somehow 'sinners' seemed offensive to such upright citizens. They were 'halfway' to faith. But how could they be taken the remainder of the way? How could they be convinced of sin, and of the need for repentance and conversion?

In a series of sermons of central importance to the Great Awakening, Edwards addressed these problems. These sermons are lengthy, even by the generous standards of his age (Edwards' inaugural sermon as president of Princeton is rumoured to have lasted two hours). Their very length, however, enabled Edwards to deal in some depth with a series of questions arising out of the two points noted above. The sermons are both critical and affirmative – critical of human ability and achievement, and affirmative of God's mercy and judgment. In that there are many remarkable parallels between Edwards' Northampton congregation of 1734 and modern western culture as a whole, it would seem worthwhile to examine his strategy.

In the first place, Edwards mounts a vigorous attack on the religious pragmatism of his day. God is not impressed by human achievements. He does not take them into account in his verdict of justification. Before justification, God regards individuals as sinners. God regards a person without faith 'only as an ungodly or wicked creature'. The judgment of the world, of American society (whether it happens to be that of eighteenth-century Northampton or modern New York), must give way to the judgment of God. For in the end it is what God makes of us that counts, not what the prevailing social ideas of morality may dictate. God judges the believer to be righteous, not on account of the *believer's* achievements, but on account of what *Christ* achieved on the cross.

At times, Edwards urges his hearers to 'seek salvation'. By doing so, he is not in any way suggesting that they can *achieve* salvation. Rather, he is urging them to recognize that salvation can only come from outside their situation.

Salvation is not something that can be attained by humans, but is something that is attained for them. For someone to seek salvation is to recognize that he or she cannot save himself or herself. It is to accept that salvation is something which that person does not yet possess. In short, it is to admit one's hopelessness and helplessness, apart from the grace of God. And here we are brought to the centre of Edwards' evangelistic strategy: the awakening of a sense of personal powerlessness in regard to salvation. With the dawning of this insight, a crucial obstacle to conversion is removed.

Secondly, Edwards insists upon the reality of human sin, a theme he would return to and develop at length in his major writing *Original Sin*. To 'half-way' Christians, the very idea of sin was offensive. The modern trend to confuse conformity to social expectations with 'righteousness' muddles the idea of sin – and many members of Edwards' Northampton congregation showed every sign of being thoroughly modern in this respect. For such people, being labelled 'a sinner' meant 'being a bad neighbour', 'being caught in an adulterous relationship', or 'adopting unacceptable business practices'. Sin had degenerated into a social idea; its reference to a relationship with God was lost.

Edwards protests powerfully against this trend. All human beings, he argues, have fallen short of the glory of God. They may conform to social conventions (at least some of the time) – but that is not the same thing as being righteous before God. It is perfectly possible to be an upright and respected citizen (or at least to be thought of in this way), while at the same time being deeply alienated from God. All of us, he insists, share an 'innate sinful depravity of the heart'. We are all in the same boat. To recognize the reality of sin is not to say that we sin all of the time; rather, it is to say that we are always prone to sin. Sin is primarily a matter of inclination, which occasionally passes into action. The state of human sin causes human acts of sin; sin causes sins.

Without this awareness of the reality and power of sin, redemption loses its relevance. The weaker your idea of sin, the poorer your understanding of salvation. If sin is understood socially, redemption comes to mean little more than being enabled to take a proper place in society. God is left out of the matter altogether. Society and its values come to take the place of God. The Northampton congregation, drawn largely from an increasingly affluent *bourgeoisie*, had a seriously deficient understanding of sin, with a correspondingly inadequate understanding of redemption. In their attitudes may be seen foreshadowed those of much of modern American culture; in Edwards' response may lie a vital challenge to that culture. A recovery of a sense of sin may be one of the most urgent tasks on the agenda of the modern theologian and preacher.

Thirdly, Edwards insists that it is only from the standpoint of faith that Christianity can be fully appreciated and understood. (A similar point was made by Augustine of Hippo, who wrote, 'Unless you believe, you will never understand.') Simply to accept the morality and truth-claims of the gospel (a position characteristic of 'halfway' Christianity) is to fail to enter into its world. With the coming of faith, all this changes: the Bible is read in a new light, and the fullness of the gospel appreciated for the first time. Edwards stresses that both head and heart, mind and emotions, are linked in faith. 'He that is spiritually enlightened ... does not merely rationally believe that God is glorious, but he has a sense of the gloriousness of God in his heart'. Before conversion, our knowledge of God is notional; after conversion, it is personal and heartfelt. Truth must be experienced in the heart as well as grasped by the mind. Assent to Christian doctrine was not enough; it was necessary to experience the presence and power of God in everyday life.

The distinction that Edwards makes at this point could be expressed in more modern terms. He is contrasting a purely cognitive understanding of God with an existential understanding. In other words, mere beliefs about God are compared unfavourably with beliefs which have been appropriated and assimilated by their believer, and which change his or her outlook on life. True knowledge of God changes people – not just their perceptions of life, but

their entire lives. Christianity is not some natural phenomenon, but is the Spirit-awakened and enlightened con-
sciousness of God's beauty, presence and power.

Unless a person has been converted, therefore, he or she
cannot fully appreciate what the gospel means. There is,
and will always be, a lack of understanding. Scripture will
not seem to relate to anything vital; the sacraments will
seem to be little more than civil ceremonies; attending
church will appear as little more than carrying out a social
duty. Morality becomes an end in itself, instead of the
natural result of faith, a duty rather than a joy. Those who
are 'half-way' to faith are thus missing out on the full riches
of the gospel, which lie beyond their grasp. Only through
conversion can the profundity of the gospel be grasped.
Accepting the truth or importance of Christianity (perhaps
as part of American culture) is one thing; being a Christian
is quite another.

Many people in modern western societies regard
Christianity as little more than a contributing element to
their culture. At best, they are prepared to pay lip service
to its ideas and values. Edwards highlights the weakness of
this position: you can never appreciate the power, the
vitality and the relevance of Christianity *from outside*. It is
only by coming to faith that the full wonder of the gospel
can be grasped. An intellectual grasp of what Christianity
is all about fails to do justice to its depth and vitality; it is
only by allowing the gospel to capture both heart and mind
that its fullness can be appreciated.

It is perhaps difficult to imagine the impact that such dry
and seemingly dull sermons must have had upon their
hearers. By modern standards, they are long and over-
involved, failing to achieve the incision and wit that many
now hold to be essential to good preaching style. Nevertheless, Edwards' sermons remain an outstanding example of
the application of the principle, 'Before God builds, he
first demolishes.' By destroying his hearers' sense of personal adequacy before God, Edwards was able to create an
atmosphere of openness and expectation, in which attention was directed towards God himself.

For many, however, the importance of Edwards lies in

the Great Awakening itself, rather than in any ideas Edwards may subsequently have developed. The Great Awakening points to the continued possibility of resurgence after periods of stagnation or decline within the churches. It points to the ability of trust in the gospel to produce changed lives and changed statistics. It points to the continuing action of the Spirit in the most unlikely situations. Early eighteenth-century New England may have seemed to many to be a spiritual desert; as Edwards' ministry demonstrates, however, the Spirit of God can make even the most arid of deserts burst into flower.

For Further Reading

The most comprehensive and readable modern biography is Iain Murray, *Jonathan Edwards*, which includes a wealth of detail on works written by or about Edwards.

The work which stimulated the current revival of interest in Edwards, especially in the United States itself, is Perry Miller, *Jonathan Edwards*.

Probably the most interesting account of Edwards' ideas yet to appear is Robert Jenson, *America's Theologian*, which demonstrates Edwards' relevance to a range of important current issues in American theology and religous life.

Yale University are in the process of producing what it is hoped will be the definitive edition of Edwards' works. To date, nine volumes have appeared. The most extensive edition currently available is the reprint of the two-volume edition of 1834.

CHAPTER TEN

KARL BARTH:

Let God be God!

THE twentieth century has yet to end; judgments concerning who its greatest theologian might be are thus
somewhat premature. Nevertheless, one of the most
powerful contenders for that title will unquestionably
be the Swiss theologian Karl Barth (1886–1968). Barth's
claim to fame rests largely on the many massive volumes of
his *Church Dogmatics*, which took the present writer four
years to read (although I was doing other things as well!)
Barth was also one of the most articulate and perceptive
critics of Adolf Hitler, and an ethical thinker of considerable merit.

Barth – the name should be pronounced to rhyme with
'cart' or 'dart' – studied theology at Berne, Berlin, Tüb-
ingen and Marburg, taking advantage of the close educational links that have always existed between Germany and
German-speaking Switzerland. During his period of theological study, Barth absorbed the ideas of liberal Protestantism, at that point the most influential German
theological movement. Although he would later react
powerfully against these ideas, there is no obvious trace of
any dissatisfaction with them in his early career.

The basic ideas of liberal Protestantism, as they were
presented by Barth's university teachers, are easily summarized. A cluster of ideas jostle for central position; perhaps most important is the idea of the evolution of human
culture. History, it is argued, is in the process of being
divinely guided towards perfection. Civilization is seen as
part of this process of evolution. In the course of human

history, a number of individuals appear who are recognized as being the bearers of special divine insights. One such individual was Jesus. By following his example and sharing in his inner life, other human beings are able to develop. The movement showed enormous and unbounded optimism in human ability and potential. Religion and culture were, it was argued, virtually identical. The term 'Culture Protestantism' became a convenient way of summarizing the beliefs of the movement.

Barth's first pastoral charge was in Geneva, as assistant minister to the German-speaking congregation in that city. In 1911 he went as pastor to the small village of Safenwil, in the Aargau region of Switzerland. Like every pastor, he was confronted with the need to deliver a sermon, Sunday after Sunday, year after year. It was not long before Barth began to become 'conscious of the responsibility to understand and interpret, and longing to fulfil it – and yet utterly incapable of doing so!' Barth would later insist that it was recognizing the need to understand and preach from the Bible that made him a proper theologian. But he initially had problems. He had difficulty in making sense of much of Scripture, on the basis of his liberal Protestant presuppositions. Something seemed to be wrong.

It has often been suggested that liberal Protestantism believed in human beings, rather than God. There is enough truth in this suggestion to make it bite. Liberal Protestantism held as fundamental a belief in the goodness of human beings and human civilization, and was optimistic concerning the future of civilization. Then something happened to shatter that faith.

In August 1914 the First World War broke out. Great European powers – all, according to liberal Protestantism, demonstrating a divinely-guided and ordained culture – began the attempt to destroy each other. Civilized nations, who were meant to demonstrate human progress and enlightenment, degenerated into barbarism in the most destructive and cruel war the world had yet seen. Liberal Protestantism's faith in the fundamental goodness of human nature and civilization began to seem absurd. To add insult to injury, Barth's former professors of theology (men whom he admired considerably) put their names to a public declaration of support for the Kaiser's war policy. For Barth, it was the end of an era.

> One day in early August 1914 stands out in my personal memory as a black day. Ninety-three German intellectuals impressed public opinion by their proclamation in support of the war policy of Kaiser Wilhelm II and his counsellors. Among these intellectuals I discovered to my horror almost all of my theological teachers whom I had greatly venerated. In despair over what this indicated about the signs of the times, I suddenly realized that I sould no longer follow either their ethics or dogmatics, or their understanding of the Bible and of history. For me at least, nineteenth century theology no longer held any future.

Liberal Protestantism had been publicly disgraced and discredited. Barth would have to rethink his whole outlook on life. This he did, night after night, in his study at Safenwil, wrestling with Scripture as he prepared for his Sunday sermons.

As the war drew to a close, Barth completed writing his first major book. It was a commentary on Paul's letter to the Romans. It wasn't a commentary in the usual sense of the word, though – Barth takes Paul's words and uses them to mount an all-out assault on what he regarded as the feeble and unrealistic outlook of liberalism. As one commentator later remarked, it was if someone had dropped a bomb into the playground of liberal theology. In this work, the easy and superficial assumptions of liberal Protestantism were set to one side, as Barth eagerly and excitedly developed the themes he found in the letter. One theme is dominant: God is God, and must be recognized as such. Where liberal Protestantism had suggested that God and humanity were close together, Barth insisted they were totally different. There was an enormous gap between them, a 'glacial crevasse'. Where liberal Protestantism suggested that God could be identified with human culture,

Barth insists that God can never, ever, be identified with anything that is human. Barth's early thought is often referred to as 'dialectical', on account of the dialectic or tension he identifies between God and humanity, the creator and his creatures. God is totally other; he is radically different; he cannot be found by human wisdom. With one swift and penetrating stroke, Barth thought that he had severed the jugular vein of liberal Protestantism. Although the ideas developed by Barth in this work would take some time to gain a full hearing, they would be warmly received by those convinced that liberalism was fatally flawed and discredited.

But how, then, do we know anything concerning God? If we cannot know God through human culture, how can we know him? If there is an unbridgeable chasm fixed between God and humanity, how can we gain access to him? This question brings us to the central theme of Barth's early thought: revelation. There is indeed an enormous gap between God and us. It is a gap which cannot be bridged from our side. Barth uses the image of the Tower of Babel to illustrate the impossibility and futility of trying to reach God from our side of the great divide. Yet the gospel declares, electrifyingly, that God has bridged this gap from his side! He has taken the initiative, stepping across the great gap of time and eternity, and making himself known in human history and in a human person. God has revealed himself in Jesus Christ. '*Dominus dixit* – the Lord has spoken' is the theme to which Barth will return time and time again. With this assertion, we move towards Barth's later theology, expressed in the *Church Dogmatics*.

In many ways, the *Romans* commentary may be regarded as a work of protest. It was like a sledgehammer – an instrument of destruction. Aided by the widespread disillusionment with liberalism following the war, Barth was able to contribute to the dismantling of its foundations without undue difficulty. It is, however, easy to destroy and criticize: to erect something better in its place is a more demanding task. After more than a decade of preparatory work, Barth rose to the challenge. In 1932 he published the first part of a work entitled *Church Dogmatics*; six million words later, Barth died at the age of eighty-one, leaving the work still uncompleted. A rumour circulating in German theological circles was thus finally and firmly quashed: 'God will allow Barth to live till it's finished – he wants to see how it ends!'

The *Church Dogmatics* is a massive attempt to explore the consequences of the fact that God has revealed himself in Jesus Christ.

> When Holy Scripture speaks of God, it concentrates our attention and thoughts upon one single point and what is to be known at that point ... And if we look closer, and ask: who and what is at this point upon which our attention and thoughts are concentrated, which we are to recognise as God, ... then from its beginning to its end, the Bible directs us to the name of Jesus Christ.

God is not something or someone who we have to find or discover, as liberal Protestantism suggested; he is the one who takes the initiative, and reveals himself to us. We do not seek God; we respond to his revelation of himself in Jesus Christ.

Barth himself once remarked, 'If I understand what I am trying to do in the *Church Dogmatics*, it is to listen to what Scripture is saying, and tell you what I hear.' Central to Barth's discussion of revelation and its relation to Scripture is the notion of the 'word of God'. Barth helpfully identifies three forms of the 'word of God', avoiding some of the confusion which sometimes centres on the notion. First, there is Jesus Christ himself, the self-revelation of God. Second, there is Holy Scripture, which is the witness to God's self-revelation in Jesus Christ. Third, there is preaching based upon Scripture, in which the word of God is proclaimed.

For Barth, Christian theology is thus based on knowledge of God as he has revealed himself in Jesus Christ; as Jesus Christ is witnessed to and interpreted by Scripture; and as scripturally-based preaching confronts us with

115

Jesus Christ. Barth was once asked about the basis of the *Church Dogmatics*. He replied: 'Its object, its source and its yardstick are . . . the *word of God*, which speaks in the Holy Scripture *to man*.' In other words, his theology concerned, was derived from and was to be judged by, the word of God as found in Scripture. 'Theology stand and falls with the word of God, for the word of God precedes all theological words by creating, arousing and challenging them.'

The theologian, Barth remarked, is like someone who walks round and round the same mountain, looking at it first from one direction, then from another. After having familiarized himself totally with what he sees, he then invites others to accompany him, as he points out its features and it beauties. His place, however, is always at the foot of that mountain. The theologian is one who goes round and round the self-revelation of God in Scripture, always remaining beneath it. He knows his place. He is someone who must learn, rather than one who knows the answers in advance. There is nothing else he need look at, other than Scripture.

> The position of theology . . . can in no wise be exalted *above* that of the biblical witnesses. The post-biblical theologian may, do doubt, possess a better astronomy, geography, zoology, psychology, physiology, and so on than these biblical witnesses possessed; but as for the word of God, he is not justified in comporting himself in relation to these witnesses as though he knew more about the word than they . . . Even the smallest, strangest, simplest or obscurest among the biblical witnesses has an incomparable advantage over even the most pious, scholarly and sagacious latter-day theologian.

(Note, incidentally, that Barth tends to treat Jesus Christ himself as *the* self-revelation of God, and Scripture as the witness to this self-revelation. He often uses the phrase 'biblical witness', as above, to make this point. This is a controversial aspect of Barth's thought, as at points Barth seems to suggest that Scripture is not *itself* revelation, but is a secondary witness to revelation.) A systematic theologian is always a scriptural theologian, willing to humble himself and be obedient to what he observes. As Calvin once remarked (and Barth would certainly agree!), 'true knowledge of God is born out of obedience'.

One area in which Barth has given considerable food for thought is the theology of preaching. What are we doing when we preach? What is the difference between a sermon and a lecture? Barth's notion of proclamation is invaluable in beginning to wrestle with such questions. Preaching concerns the proclamation of Jesus Christ – in other words, with the declaration of who Jesus Christ is and what his relevance to us might be. Preaching makes demands of us in the name of Jesus Christ. It confronts us with Jesus Christ, and obliges us to wrestle with what his will for us might be. To those outside the church, Jesus Christ is proclaimed as saviour and Lord, the one who demands and deserves their obedience. Evangelism is thus the proclamation of Jesus Christ. But to those within the church, Jesus Christ is also proclaimed as saviour and Lord, the one who has won their obedience, and who now invites further consideration of what form this obedience might take.

Preaching also provides a vital stimulus for thought. It invites the believer to think through his or her faith. Anselm of Canterbury introduced the phrase 'faith seeking understanding (*fides quaerens intellectum*)' to make this point: when an individual comes to faith, it is natural and proper that he or she should want to *understand* what they believe. Barth uses this idea and this phrase to explain the purpose of theology. 'The faith of the community is asked to seek understanding. Faith seeking understanding, *fides quaerens intellectum*, is what theology must embody and represent. What distinguishes faith from blind assent is just its special character as "faith seeking understanding".'

Barth's stress upon the importance of preaching derives from his conviction that it is here that God *acts*. Through the proclamation of the word of God, the church and the world are forced to hear that word and respond to it. The function of theology is *critical*, in that it is obliged to ensure that the church's proclamation remains faithful to the word of God, expressed in Scripture, to which it bears witness. But it is also *positive*, in that theology is also written from the standpoint of faith as a function of the church. Barth thus puts academic theology in its proper context: it is a good servant, but a poor master.

But who is the theologian? Some professional who lectures at a university? For Barth, theology is far too important to be left to such people. It is a matter for everyone who believes, and thinks about his or her faith. It is a matter for anyone who wants to think responsibly about God, and the tasks and opportunities which faith in God brings.

> Theology is not a private subject for theologians only. Nor is it a private subject for professors. Fortunately, there have always been pastors who have understood more about theology than most professors. Nor is theology a private subject of study for pastors. Fortunately, there have repeatedly been congregation members, and often whole congregations, who have pursued theology energetically while their pastors were theological infants or barbarians. Theology is a matter for the Church.

For Barth, the mission of the church, the basis of its proclamation, worship and adoration, is none other than the word of God in its three-fold form: in Jesus Christ, in Scripture, and in the proclamation of the church. It is those entrusted with the exposition of Scripture, with the proclamation of the word of God and with the criticism of the doctrine and practice of the Christian church upon their basis, who should be recognized as theologians. 'The task of theology consists in again and again reminding the people in the Church, both preachers and congregations, that the life and work of the Church are under the authority of the gospel and the law, that God should be heard.' The recognition of the centrality of Jesus Christ to Christian theology involves the demand that the life and doctrine of the church should be critically evaluated on the basis of Scripture, and Scripture alone. The pastor's study and pulpit are essential elements within this process, which cannot be dismissed or marginalized by those who regard themselves as 'theological professionals'. To be a theologian is to be a preacher of the word of God. True to his own principles, Barth continued to preach regularly after he left parish ministry and became a professor of theology. Some of his finest sermons were preached to convicts at Basle jail!

While a pastor at Safenwil, Barth himself had agonized over the responsibilities of preaching. How could he be sure that the words he spoke had the authority of God? How could he avoid presenting his own ideas, as if they had divine authority? How could he tell the difference between the word of God and the words of Karl Barth? Gradually, the idea of fidelity and obedience to Scripture emerged as the key to his dilemma: the true theologian and preacher is the one who *listens* to the word of God, who is captive to that word, and who is its humble servant. Again, Barth remained faithful to these insights, especially while teaching in Nazi Germany. At the height of the Nazi rise to power in the 1930s, Barth declared that the *only* voice that Christians should heed is that of Jesus Christ. Where others in Germany were seduced by the rhetoric of Adolf Hitler, Barth insisted that only one individual could stand at the centre of the Christian life – Jesus Christ himself. 'Jesus Christ, as he is attested for us in Holy Scripture, is the one Word of God which we have to hear and which we have to trust and obey in life and in death.'

It is insights such as these which establish Barth's importance as a leading Christian thinker, rather than merely as an academic theologian. For Barth, theology is intimately concerned with preaching, with the proclamation of Jesus Christ, with the well-being and life of the church in the world. It is theology which undergirds the life and doctrine of the church, as a discipline which is exercised by that church as a totality. Some academic theologians virtually suggested that nothing could be said about God without their permission. This 'papacy of the professors' is rejected by Barth as implying a false understanding of the nature of theology itself. Theology is an enterprise undertaken by believers within the community of faith, as they pray and reflect upon their faith.

> The task which is laid upon theology, and which it can and should fulfil, is its service in the church, to the Lord of the church. It has its definite function in the church's liturgy, that is, in the various phases of the church's expression: in every reverent proclamation of the gospel, or in every proclaiming reverence, in which the church listens and attends to God. Theology does not exist in a vacuum, nor in any arbitrarily selected field, but in that province between baptism and communion, in the realm between the Scriptures and their exposition and proclamation.

Just as Luther proclaimed the 'priesthood of all believers', so Barth proclaims the theological competence of all believers. And just as Luther insisted that the 'priesthood of all believers' did not abolish the ordained ministry, but merely set it in its proper context, so Barth emphasizes the need to maintain a proper link between theology and faith, between the theologian and the believer. The theologian cannot be allowed to set his own agenda, following his own methods, in that these have already been selected, not *by* him, but *for* him. It is the context of worship, adoration, preaching, mission and proclamation which defines the parameters within which theology operates – all of which directly concern the life and doctrine of the church and the ordinary believer. Barth's views may appear to be anti-intellectual, but it is evident that Barth's protests are directed entirely against a false concept of theology itself. Theology is a function of the church – it is a committed discipline, whose service is to the Lord of the church, and whose servants are those – whoever they may be – who are obedient hearers of the word of God.

For Barth, then, theology is a discipline which requires obedience and humility. The theologian's place is *under* the Word of God; the theologian is *judged by* that Word, and is not in any position to *judge* that Word. In the end, we must realize that God is God, and that our human words and concepts can never do justice to him. Human words, ideas and institutions may point to God – but they may never be identified with him. In this way, Barth encourages every generation to rediscover for themselves the *otherness* of God, to experience the overwhelming sense of the *divinity* of God, and to respond in humility, obedience and wonder.

In closing this chapter, it must be stressed that Barth is a controversial figure, who is often regarded as being an inadequate exponent of many traditional Christian doctrines. For example, his views on redemption are generally thought to amount to universal salvation – the belief that everyone will eventually be saved, whether or not they want to be. This would certainly seem to be inconsistent with many passages in the New Testament. Nevertheless, Barth has been included in the present work, on account of his importance and the simple fact that he is so *stimulating*. If I may add a personal note, Barth is one of the few theologians who makes me want to rise from reading him, and preach a sermon there and then! So read him and enjoy him – but be prepared to criticize him as well. After all, Barth insisted that *you*, as a faithful reader of Scripture, have just as much right to be a theologian as anyone else.

For Further Reading

The most detailed biography of Barth currently available is E. Busch, *Karl Barth*. In addition to valuable material on Barth's theological development, this work includes important material on Barth's opposition to Hitler.

General introductions to Barth's thought of particular interest include: G. W. Bromiley, *Introduction to the Theology of Karl Barth*, and T. H. L. Parker, *Karl Barth*. Both these works are written by scholars involved in the translation of Barth's *Church Dogmatics* into English. Bromiley is the more detailed, while Parker is perhaps easier to read.

For more detailed studies of Barth's thought, suitable for more advanced readers, see: *Reckoning with Barth*, ed. Nigel Biggar, a useful collection of essays on the main themes of Barth's thought, with particular emphasis upon his ethics; and Robert Jenson, *Alpha and Omega*, a stimulating analysis by a leading American interpreter of Barth.

Barth's massive output makes it difficult to know where to begin reading. However, the following work is usually singled out as one of several jewels in his literary crown: Barth, *Evangelical Theology*. Originally given as a series of lectures at Princeton, this book scintillates with insights on the nature of theology, and its relation to Jesus Christ, Scripture and preaching. Easy to read, the lectures are in many ways a classic statement of Barth's mature position. It is difficult to avoid a sense of excitement on reading this work.

For a taste of Barth writing in a more systematic and measured manner, try dipping into one of the many published 'samplers' of the *Church Dogmatics*.

The *Romans* commentary, although difficult to read, allows one to sample Barth in his 'dialectical' phase. The comments on Romans 1:16–17 (pp. 35–42) or 2:1–5 (pp. 56–61) are excellent samples of his early critique of liberalism.

CHAPTER ELEVEN

C. S. LEWIS:

Longing for God

CLIVE Staples Lewis – 'Jack' to his friends – was born in Belfast, Northern Ireland on 29 November 1898. His father was a successful solicitor, who was doing well enough to allow the family to move to a large house ('Little Lea') on the outskirts of Belfast in 1905. Shortly afterwards, Lewis's mother died, leaving his father to look after Lewis and his elder brother Warren. The two brothers spent hours alone in the vast attic of the old house, inhabiting imaginary worlds of their own making.

If Lewis ever had any Christian faith to start with, he soon lost it. After a period serving in the British Army during the First World War, Lewis went up to Oxford. He was a student at University College in the period 1919–1923, taking first class honours in Greats (classics and philosophy) in 1922, and first class honours in English the following year. After a period during which his future seemed uncertain, he was elected a fellow of Magdalen College in the spring of 1925. He would remain at the college until 1954, when he was invited to take up the newly-created chair of Medieval and Renaissance English at Cambridge. The chair was linked with a fellowship at Magdalene College, Cambridge. (As his extensive correspondence indicates, Lewis took some pleasure in pointing out the verbal link between his old and new colleges.) Lewis died at his Oxford home at 5.30 p.m. on 22 November 1963, a few hours before the world was shocked by the news of the assassination of President John F. Kennedy at Dallas, Texas.

During the 1920s, Lewis had time to reconsider his attitude to Christianity. The story of his return to the faith he abandoned as a boy is described in great detail in his autobiography, *Surprised by Joy*. After wrestling with the clues concerning God he found in human reason and experience, he eventually decided that intellectual honesty compelled him to believe and trust in God. He did not want to; he felt, however, that he had no choice. The passage in *Surprised by Joy* describing this great moment of decision has become famous:

> You must picture me alone in that room at Magdalen, night after night, feeling, whenever my mind lifted even for a second from my work, the steady unrelenting approach of Him whom I so earnestly desired not to meet. That which I greatly feared had at last come upon me. In the Trinity Term of 1929 I gave in, and admitted that God was God, and knelt and prayed: perhaps, that night, the most dejected and reluctant convert in all England. I did not then see what is now the most shining and obvious thing; the divine humility which will accept a convert even on such terms. The Prodigal Son at least walked home on his own feet. But who can duly adore that Love which will open the high gates to a prodigal who is brought in kicking, struggling, resentful, and darting his eyes in every direction for a chance of escape?

After his conversion, Lewis began to establish his reputation as a leading authority on Medieval and Renaissance English literature. *The Allegory of Love*, published in 1936, is still regarded as a masterpiece, as is his *Preface to Paradise Lost*. Alongside his scholarly writings, however, Lewis wrote books of a very different nature. Aiming at clarity and conviction, Lewis produced a series of works aimed at communicating the reasonableness of Christianity to his own generation. The works brought him popular acclaim, but seemed to some to destroy his scholarly reputation. In 1946, he was passed over for the Merton professorship of English Literature at Oxford.

The first popular book was *The Pilgrim's Regress*, based loosely on John Bunyan's *Pilgrim's Progress*. It was not a success. Nevertheless, Lewis continued. *The Problem of Pain* appeared in 1940. It was well received, and on the basis of its clarity and intelligence of argument, Lewis was invited to give a series of radio talks by the British Broadcasting Corporation. In 1942, these were published as *The Case for Christianity*. Such was their success that Lewis combined them with two other short works – *Christian Behaviour* (1943) and *Beyond Personality* (1944) – to yield *Mere Christianity*. 1942 also saw the publication of *The Screwtape Letters*, whose wit and insight firmly established Lewis reputation as a leading defender of the Christian faith.

That reputation was consolidated by further works, including *Miracles* (1947) and *The Four Loves* (1960). Outspokenly critical of 'Christianity-and-water' (as he dubbed liberal versions of Christianity), he struck a deep chord of sympathy with his readers. The critics were furious. Alistair Cooke described him as a 'very unremarkable minor prophet', who would soon be forgotten once the Second World War had ended – a prediction in which Cooke showed himself to be a very unremarkable and incompetent minor prophet.

Professional theologians were also irritated at Lewis's success, and accused him of simplifying things; Lewis responded by suggesting that, if professional theologians had done their job properly, there would be no need for lay theologians such as himself. His death in 1963 did nothing to stem the growing tide of interest in his writings. In April 1980, *Time* magazine reported that Lewis was unquestionably 'this century's most-read apologist for God'. Even after his death, his influence lives on; thousands who never knew Lewis in the flesh attribute their discovery of, or return to, Christianity to the influence of his writings.

What is it about those writings which possesses such an appeal to so many? Unquestionably, it is Lewis's intelligent and persuasive approach to Christianity. For Lewis, Christianity makes sense. It commends itself by its reasonableness. Believing in God makes more sense, Lewis argued, than not believing in him. *Mere Christianity* is perhaps as outstanding an example of a lucid and intelligent presentation of the rational and moral case for Christian belief as we are ever likely to see.

Yet there is more to Lewis than this. Alongside Lewis the cool-headed thinker we find a very different style of thinker – a man who is aware of the power of the human imagination, and the implications of this power for our understanding of reality. Perhaps one of the most original aspects of Lewis's writing is his persistent and powerful appeal to the religious imagination. Lewis was aware of certain deep human emotions which pointed to a dimension of our existence beyond time and space. There is, Lewis suggested, a deep and intense feeling of longing within human beings, which no earthly object or experience can satisfy. Lewis terms this sense 'joy', and argues that it points to God as its source and goal (hence the title of his autobiography).

To understand Lewis at this point, the idea of 'joy' needs to be explained in some detail. From the windows of his home in Belfast, the young Lewis could see the distant Castlereagh Hills. These far-off hills seemed to symbolize something which lay beyond his reach. A sense of intense longing arose as he contemplated them. He could not say exactly *what* it was that he longed for; merely that there was a sense of emptiness within him, which the mysterious hills seemed to heighten, without satisfying. In *The Pilgrim's Regress*, these hills appear as a symbol of the heart's unknown desire.

Lewis describes this experience (perhaps better known to students of German Romanticism as *Sehnsucht*) in some detail in his autobiography. He relates how, as a young child, he was standing by a flowering currant bush, when – for some unexplained reason – a memory was triggered off.

> There suddenly rose in me without warning, as if from a depth not of years but of centuries, the memory of that earlier morning at the Old House when my brother had brought his toy garden into

the nursery. It is difficult to find words strong enough for the sensation which came over me; Milton's 'enormous bliss' of Eden ... comes somewhere near it. It was a sensation, of course, of desire; but desire for what? Not, certainly, for a biscuit tin filled with moss, nor even (though that came into it) for my own past ... and before I knew what I desired, the desire itself was gone, the whole glimpse withdrawn, the world turned commonplace again, or only stirred by a longing for the longing that had just ceased. It had only taken a moment of time; and in a certain sense everything else that had ever happened to me was insignificant in comparison.

Lewis here describes a brief moment of insight, a devastating moment of feeling caught up in something which goes far beyond the realms of everyday experience. But what did it mean? What, if anything, did it point to?

Lewis addressed this question in a remarkable sermon entitled 'The Weight of Glory', preached on 8 June 1941. Lewis spoke of 'a desire which no natural happiness will satisfy', 'a desire, still wandering and uncertain of its object and still largely unable to see that object in the direction where it really lies'. There is something self-defeating about human desire, in that what is desired, when achieved, seems to leave the desire unsatisfied. Lewis illustrates this from the age-old quest for beauty.

The books or the music in which we thought the beauty was located will betray us if we trust to them; it was not *in* them, it only came *through* them, and what came through them was longing. These things – the beauty, the memory of our own past – are good images of what we really desire; but if they are mistaken for the thing itself they turn into dumb idols, breaking the hearts of their worshippers. For they are not the thing itself; they are only the scent of a flower we have not found, the echo of a tune we have not heard, news from a country we have not visited.

Human desire, the deep and bitter-sweet longing for something that will satisfy us, points beyond finite objects and finite persons (who seem able to fulfil this desire, yet eventually prove incapable of doing so); it points *through* these objects, and persons towards their real goal and fulfilment in God himself.

A similar pattern is observed with human personal relationships. In love, perhaps the deepest human relationship of all, we encounter the strange longing to lose ourselves in another – to enter into a relationship which paradoxically simultaneously heightens and obliterates our own identity. Yet even love, which seems to offer all, delivers less than it seems to promise. Somehow in personal relationships there is to be found a bitter-sweet longing – something which *comes through* the relationship, but is not actually *in* that relationship. Evelyn Waugh's novel *Brideshead Revisited* captures the frustration of so much personal experience, whether in the quest for love or the quest for beauty. Somehow, that quest always fails to find its object. Even when the search seems close to its end, we find we have yet another corner to turn. Whatever it is that we are pursuing remains elusively ahead of us, evading our grasp.

> Perhaps all our loves are merely hints and symbols; vagabond-language scratched on gateposts and paving-stones along the weary road that others have tramped before us; perhaps you and I are types and this sadness which sometimes falls between us springs from disappointment in our search, each straining through and beyond the other, snatching a glimpse now and then of the shadow, which turns the corner always a pace or two ahead of us.

It is as if human love points to something beyond it, as a parable. The paradox of hedonism – the simple, yet stultifying, fact that pleasure cannot satisfy – is another instance of this curious phenomenon. Pleasure, beauty, personal relationships: all seem to promise so much, and yet when we grasp them, we find that what we were seeking was not located in them, but lies beyond them.

There is a 'divine dissatisfaction' within human experience, which prompts us to ask whether there is anything which may satisfy the human quest to fulfil the desires of the human heart.

Lewis argues that there is. Hunger, he suggests, is an excellent example of a human sensation which corresponds to a real physical need. This need points to the existence of food by which it may be met. Thirst is an example of a human longing pointing to a human need, which in turn points to its fulfilment in drinking. Any human longing, he argues, points to a genuine human need, which in turn points to a real object corresponding to that need. A similar point is made, although a little cryptically, in relation to human sexual desire. And so, Lewis suggests, it is reasonable to suggest that the deep human sense of infinite longing which cannot be satisfied by any physical or finite object or person must point to a real human need which can, in some way, be met.

This point is made clearly in a letter to his brother, dated 31 October 1931.

The 'idea of God' in *some* minds does contain, not a mere abstract definition, but real imaginative perception of goodness and beauty, beyond their own resources, and this not only in minds which already believe in God. It certainly seems to me that the 'vague something' which has been suggested to one's mind as desirable, all one's life, in experiences of nature and music and poetry, even in such ostensibly irreligious forms as the 'land east of the Sun and west of the Moon' in Morris, and which arouses desires that no finite object even pretends to satisfy, can be argued *not* to be any product of our own imagination.

In other words, the sense of 'desires that no finite object even pretends to satisfy' corresponds to a real human need, and the fulfilment of that need – but how?

Lewis argues that this sense of longing points to its origin and its fulfilment in God himself. In this, he echoes a great theme of traditional Christian thinking about the origin and goal of human nature. 'You have made us for yourself, O Lord, and our hearts are restless until they find their rest in you' (Augustine of Hippo). We are made by God, and we experience a deep sense of longing for him, which only he can satisfy. Although Lewis's reflections on the desire he calls 'joy' reflect his personal experience, it is evident that he (and countless others) consider that this sense of longing is a widespread feature of human nature and experience. An important point of contact for the proclamation of the gospel is thus established.

Lewis's insights also bring new depth to familiar biblical passages concerning human longing for God. 'As the deer pants for streams of water, so my soul pants for you, O God. My soul thirsts for God, the living God' (Ps. 42:1). Note the great sense of *longing* for God expressed in this verse – a sense of longing which assumes added meaning if Lewis's reflections on 'joy' are allowed. Note also the biblical parallel between a sense of need – in this case, animal thirst – and the human need and desire for God.

But is this transcendent object of desire *real*? Lewis suggests that the pursuit of the clues offered by human desire only makes sense if there is a fourth dimension to human existence, served by the human imagination. The 'watchful dragon' of human reason is hesitant to allow us to speak of anything which goes beyond experience. In order to deal with this question, Lewis turns to Plato's analogy of the cave. In his hands, this familiar image is transformed into a persuasive and powerful tool for relating the world of experience and the world that lies beyond it and through it – which Lewis identifies with God.

As Plato uses the analogy, we are asked to think of a group of men who are confined to a cave. A fire is burning, and they see shadows thrown on to the wall of the cave. The cave is the only world they have ever experienced, and so they naturally assume that it is the real world – the *only* world. The shadows they see are all that there is to reality. Then one of the men escapes from the cave, and discovers the great world outside; he returns to tell the others, who cannot believe him. Can there really be another world, which transcends the one they know from experience?

Lewis develops this analogy in *The Silver Chair*, one of the *Chronicles of Narnia*. In this book, a Narnian finds himself confronted by a witch in an underground kingdom. The witch attempts to persuade him that the underground kingdom is the real world – that it is the *only* world. The Narnian is not impressed. Knowing that she is wrong, however, he has to persuade her to enlarge her mental horizons. His argument is telling.

> Suppose we *have* only dreamed, or made up, all those things – trees and grass and sun and moon and stars and Aslan himself. Suppose we have. Then all I can say is that, in that case, the made-up things seem a good deal more important than the real ones. Suppose this black pit of a kingdom of yours *is* the only world. Well, it strikes me as a pretty poor one. And that's a funny thing, when you come to think of it. We're just babies playing a game, if you're right. But four babies playing a game can make a play-world which licks your world hollow.

The argument here is a classic, having its origins in the Greek fathers, and finding its mature expression in Thomas Aquinas: if certain ideas in our minds cannot be accounted for on the basis of our experience of the world, they must be accounted for in terms of something beyond that world. The apparently 'real' world must be supplemented by another world, an 'imagined world' – not in the sense of an *invented* world, but a *real* world into which we must enter by our imagination.

But there remains the possibility that this 'imagined world' is an invented world. Religious ideas might just be based upon everyday notions. God could just be modelled on an earthly king or father, much enlarged. The reality, it might be argued, lies in the present world; the analogous idea is imaginary. Human fathers are real; God the father

is an human invention. Lewis deals with this question at
several points, perhaps most memorably in *The Silver
Chair*. The witch invites a Narnian prince to tell her about
what he calls 'the sun'. There is no equivalent in the under-
world to which she belongs. The prince replies by con-
structing an analogy: the sun is like a lamp.

> 'You see that lamp. It is round and yellow and gives
> light to the whole room; and hangeth moreover
> from the roof. Now that thing which we call the sun
> is like the lamp, only far greater and brighter. It
> giveth light to the whole Overworld and hangeth in
> the sky.'
>   'Hangeth from what, my Lord?', asked the witch;
> and then, while they were all still thinking how to
> answer her, she added, with another of her soft,
> silver laughs, 'You see? When you try to think out
> clearly what this *sun* must be, you cannot tell me.
> You can only tell me that it is like the lamp. Your *sun*
> is a dream; and there is nothing in that dream that
> was not copied from the lamp. The lamp is the real
> thing; the *sun* is but a tale, a children's story.'

In other words, the sun is an imagined and invented
notion, based on a real object – a lamp.

Knowing that his readers are perfectly aware that the
sun really exists, Lewis is thus able to demonstrate the
superficial sophistication of the witch's argument: it seems
clever and persuasive, but is actually seriously wrong. God
is not just based on human figures (such as a shepherd,
ruler or father), but is an independent existence in his own
right. Human figures are able to mirror him to some
extent; this analogy, however, does not imply God's non-
existence! Throughout his writings, Lewis stresses the correspondence between human longings and their satisfaction through an encounter with the living God.

Perhaps the finest statement of the theological implications of this deep sense of longing is to be found in *Till
We Have Faces*, Lewis's brilliant retelling of the love story
between Cupid and Psyche. In one passage, Lewis has

Psyche tell her sister (who here relates the story) of her longing for something which she senses lies beyond the world as she experiences it.

'I have always – at least, ever since I can remember – had a longing for death.'

'Ah, Psyche,' I said, 'have I made you so little happy as that?'

'No, no, no,' she said. 'You don't understand. Not that kind of longing. It was when I was happiest that I longed most. It was on happy days, when we were up there on the hills, the three of us, with the wind and the sunshine . . . Do you remember? The colour and the smell, and looking across at the Grey Mountain in the distance? And because it was so beautiful, it set me longing, always longing. Somewhere else there must be more of it. Everything seemed to be saying, Psyche come! But I couldn't (not yet) come and I didn't know where I was to come to. It almost hurt me. I felt like a bird in a cage when the other birds of its kind are flying home.'

Psyche's experience of a sense of longing for something indefinable, evoked by the beauty of the world, ends in frustration; nothing in the world can satisfy her longing. It is only by being set free from the limitations of the world itself that Psyche can experience the fulfilment of her sense of longing. And so our hearts are also restless, until they find their rest in the God who created us for fellowship with him.

There is more to Lewis – and, indeed, to all the theologians discussed in this work – than it is possible to examine in this very brief chapter. Nevertheless, it is hoped that this account of Lewis will stimulate you to read more by him and about him; as, indeed, it may so stimulate you in relation to the other writers discussed.

For Further Reading

Lewis's account of his early life and conversion is contained in *Surprised by Joy*. Other biographies (such as those listed below) may enlarge this work at points of detail, but fail to capture its atmosphere of exploration and joyful discovery.

Roger Lancelyn Green and Walter Hooper, *C. S. Lewis: A Biography*. A fine study of Lewis's career, with much important material on his conversion and development as a Christian.

William Griffin, *C. S. Lewis: The Authentic Voice*. A biography which draws extensively on Lewis's own writings, many of them obscure or unpublished.

Lewis's distinctive approach to Christianity is probably best illustrated from the following four works: *Mere Christianity*; *Miracles*; *The Problem of Pain*; *The Screwtape Letters*.

The sermon 'The Weight of Glory' is a brief yet classic exposition of his appeal to the imagination.

Richard L. Purtill, *C. S. Lewis's Case for the Christian Faith*. An excellent introduction to the main themes of Lewis's thought.

Chad Walsh, *C. S. Lewis: Apostle to the Sceptics*. An early study of Lewis's defence of the Christian faith. Although restricted to works published in the 1930s and 1940s, this is an excellent study of the man and his literary mission.

Chad Walsh, *The Literary Legacy of C. S. Lewis*. A stimulating study of the way in which Lewis uses literature and literary devices – including the appeal to the imagination – in developing the case for the Christian faith.

WHERE NEXT?

IF you found some of the writers and ideas explored in this work interesting, you may be wondering where to go next. Three brief suggestions may be made.

First, you might like to consider looking at additional writers. An excellent addition to the list would be the twentieth-century writer Francis Schaeffer, whose writings on the relation between Christianity and modern western culture are thought by many to be outstanding. Or ask your friends which Christian writers they find helpful – and why!

Second, consider sticking with the writers discussed in the present work. As you have now become familiar with them, you could explore other areas of their writings, with a view to stimulating your thinking on other topics. Two areas of potential interest to many readers are the problem of evil (discussed particularly well by Augustine and C. S. Lewis), and the relation of the believer to secular society (treated by Augustine, Calvin and Barth). If you follow up the suggested reading, you may well come across other topics of interest covered by these writers, and be moved to follow them up.

Third, you may feel like looking at one area of Christian thought in some detail, developing some of the ideas you met in this work. Three areas are especially suitable at this stage, and are well served with suitable reading material at an introductory level. These are the doctrine of the person of Christ (Christology); the doctrine of the work of Christ (soteriology, or the doctrine of the Atonement); and the doctrine of God (especially the doctrine of the Trinity). Further study of any of these will lend added depth to your thinking and strength to your faith.

For Further Reading

Francis Schaeffer is a prolific writer, whose many writings have been gathered together in the five volumes of *Complete Works: A Christian Worldview*. Of particular interest are his *Escape from Reason* and *The God Who is There*. Available as individual works, these are also brought together in volume 1 of the *Complete Works*. A helpful introduction to the many aspects of Schaeffer's Christian worldview is provided by the collection of essays in Ronald W. Ruegsegger (ed.), *Reflections on Francis Schaeffer*.

The problem of evil can be studied from a number of works. G. R. Evans, *Augustine on Evil*, is a helpful analysis of Augustine's discussion of evil, setting it in the context of his thought in general. C. S. Lewis, *The Problem of Pain*, is an excellent discussion of the subject.

The relation between faith and secular society can be studied from the following books. R. A. Markus, *Saeculum: History and Society in the Theology of St Augustine*, is an advanced discussion of Augustine's account of the relation of the church and political power and structures. Although it is difficult reading at points, it is well worth the effort.

Harro Höpfl, *The Christian Polity of John Calvin*, is an excellent account of Calvin's views on the way in which Christian faith should express itself in social and political structures. Written with particular reference to Calvin's Geneva, it illustrates how Calvin was able to anchor the gospel in this specific historical situation.

The area of Christology (that is, the person of Jesus Christ), is best approached through introductory texts, such as A. McGrath, *Understanding Jesus*. Once you have become familiar with the basic ideas, you can explore them further, with reference to such texts as: C. F. D. Moule, *The Origins of Christology*, an excellent study of the New Testament understandings of Jesus; and Alister McGrath, *The Making of Modern German Christology*, a useful summary of the main developments in German-language Christology from the Enlightenment to the modern period.

The area of the work of Christ can also be approached through introductory texts such as McGrath, *Understanding Jesus*. However, an ideal work for further study of this crucial area of Christian thought is: J. R. W. Stott, *The Cross of Christ*, a superb analysis of the meaning of the death of Jesus Christ.

The doctrine of God can be approached easily through introductory works such as A. McGrath, *Understanding the Trinity*. More advanced works on this theme include: Tom Smail, *The Forgotten Father*, a marvellous study of the fatherhood of God; Ronald H. Nash, *The Concept of God*, a useful analysis of some contemporary problems with aspects of the Christian doctrine of God; and E. Calvin Beisner, *God in Three Persons*, which includes a helpful discussion of the history of the doctrine of the Trinity.

FOR FURTHER READING

Primary Sources

Karl Barth, *The Epistle to the Romans*. Translated by Edwyn C. Hoskyns (Oxford: Oxford University Press, 1968).

—, *Church Dogmatics* (13 vols: Edinburgh: Clark, 1956–1975).

—, *Evangelical Theology* (London: Weidenfeld & Nicholson, 1968).

John Calvin, *The Institutes of the Christian Religion*. Translated by F. L. Battles. (2 vols: Philadelphia: Westminster Press, 1961).

Jonathan Edwards, *Works* (2 vols: Carlisle, Pa.: Banner of Truth, 1974).

—, *Works* (7 vols: New Haven: Yale University Press, 1957–1985).

C. S. Lewis, *Mere Christianity* (New York: Macmillan, 1952).

—, *Miracles* (New York: Macmillan, 1947).

—, *The Problem of Pain* (New York: Macmillan, 1943).

—, *The Screwtape Letters* (New York: Macmillan, 1962).

—, 'The Weight of Glory', in *The Weight of Glory and Other Addresses* (NewYork: Macmillan, 1980).

Francis Schaeffer, *Escape from Reason* (Downers Grove, Ill.: InterVarsity Press, 1968).

—, *The God Who is There* (Downers Grove, Ill.: InterVarsity Press, 1968).

—, *Complete Works: A Christian Worldview* (5 vols: Westchester, Ill.: Crossway, 1982).

Secondary Sources

Roland H. Bainton, *Here I Stand: A Life of Martin Luther* (New York: Abingdon Press, 1950).

F. L. Battles, 'God Was Accommodating Himself to Human Capacity', *Interpretation* 31 (1977), pp. 19–38.

E. Calvin Beisner, *God in Three Persons* (Wheaton, Ill.: Tyndale Press, 1984).

Nigel Biggar, (ed.), *Reckoning with Barth* (Oxford: Mowbray, 1988).

Gerald Bonner, *Augustine of Hippo: Life and Controversies* (Philadelphia: Westminster Press, 1963).

Gerald Bray, *Creeds, Councils and Christ* (Downers Grove, Ill.: InterVarsity Press, 1984).

G. W. Bromiley, *An Introduction to the Theology of Karl Barth* (Edinburgh: Clark, 1980).

Colin Brown, *History & Faith: A Personal Exploration* (Grand Rapids, Mich.: Zondervan, 1987).

Colin Brown, *Philosophy and the Christian Faith* (Downers Grove, Ill.: InterVarsity Press, 1986).

Peter Brown, *Augustine of Hippo: A Biography* (Berkeley: University of California Press, 1967).

Eberhard Busch, *Karl Barth: A Biography* (London: SCM Press, 1976).

Henry Chadwick, *The Early Church* (Baltimore: Penguin Books, 1967).

—, *Augustine* (Oxford: Oxford University Press, 1986).

F. C. Coplestone, *Aquinas* (Harmondsworth: Penguin, 1967).

G. R. Evans, *Augustine on Evil* (Cambridge: Cambridge University Press, 1980).

—, *Anselm* (London: Geoffrey Chapman Publishers, 1989).

Alexandre Ganoczy, *The Young Calvin* (Edinburgh: Clark, 1988).

Roger L. Green, and Walter Hooper, *C. S. Lewis: A Biography* (New York: Harcourt Brace Jovanovich, 1976).

William Griffin, *C. S. Lewis: The Authentic Voice* (Batavia, Ill.: Lion Publishing Corporation, 1986).

Egli Grislis, 'Calvin's Use of Cicero in the Institutes I: 1–5 – A Case Study in Theological Method', *Archiv für Refor-*

mationsgeschichte 62 (1971), pp. 5–37.

R. P. C. Hanson, *In search of the Christian Doctrine of God: The Arian Controversy 318–381* (Edinburgh: Clark, 1988).

Harro Höpfl, *The Christian Polity of John Calvin* (Cambridge: Cambridge University Press, 1982).

Robert W. Jenson, *Alpha and Omega: A Study in the Theology of Karl Barth* (New York: Nelson, 1963).

—, *America's Theologian: A Recommendation of Jonathan Edwards* (New York: Oxford University Press, 1988).

James M. Kittelson, *Luther the Reformer: The Story of the Man and His Career* (Minneapolis: Ausburg Publishing House, 1986).

Walter von Loewenich, *Martin Luther: The Man and His Work* (Minneapolis: Augsburg Publishing House, 1986).

Bernhard Lohse, *Martin Luther: An Introduction to His Life and Work* (Philadelphia: Fortress Press, 1986).

Alister E. McGrath, *Luther's Theology of the Cross: Martin Luther's Theological Breakthrough* (Oxford/New York: Basil Blackwell, 1985).

—, *Understanding Jesus* (Grand Rapids, Mich.: Zondervan, 1987).

—, *Understanding the Trinity* (Grand Rapids, Mich.: Zondervan, 1988).

—, *The Making of Modern German Christology* (Oxford/New York: Basil Blackwell, 1986).

—, *The Mystery of the Cross* (Grand Rapids, Mich.: Zondervan, 1988).

—, *Justification by Faith: An Introduction* (Grand Rapids, Mich.: Zondervan, 1988).

—, *Explaining Your Faith* (Grand Rapids, Mich.: Zondervan, 1989).

—, *Reformation Thought: An Introduction* (Oxford/New York: Basil Blackwell, 1988).

—, *The Sunnier Side of Doubt* (Grand Rapids, Mich.: Zondervan, 1990).

R. A. Markus, *Saeculum: History and Society in the Theology of St Augustine* (Cambridge: Cambridge University Press, 1970).

Perry Miller, *Jonathan Edwards* (New York: Sloane, 1949).

Jürgen Moltmann, *The Crucified God: The Cross of Christ as the Foundation and Criticism of Christian Theology* (New

York: Harper & Row, 1974).

C. F. D. Moule, *The Origin of Christology* (Cambridge: Cambridge University Press, 1978).

Iain H. Murray, *Jonathan Edwards: A New Biography* (Carlisle, Pa.: Banner of Truth, 1988).

Ronald H. Nash, *The Concept of God* (Grand Rapids, Mich.: Zondervan, 1983).

T. H. L. Parker, *Karl Barth* (Grand Rapids, Mich.: Eerdmans, 1970).

—, *John Calvin* (Batavia, Ill.: Lion Publishing Corporation, 1987).

E. Persson, *Sacra Doctrina: Reason and Revelation in Aquinas* (Oxford: Basil Blackwell, 1970).

G. R. Potter, *Zwingli* (Cambridge: Cambridge University Press, 1976).

Menna Prestwich, (ed.), *International Calvinism 1541–1715* (Oxford: Oxford University Press, 1985).

Richard L. Purtill, *C. S. Lewis's Case for the Christian Faith* (San Francisco: Harper & Row, 1985).

Ronald W. Ruegsegger, (ed.), *Reflections on Francis Schaeffer* (Grand Rapids, Mich.: Zondervan, 1986).

Tom Smail, *The Forgotten Father* (London: Hodder & Stoughton, 1988).

W. P. Stephens, *The Theology of Huldrych Zwingli* (Oxford: Oxford University Press, 1986).

Chad Walsh, *C. S. Lewis: Apostle to the Sceptics* (New York: Macmillan, 1949).

—, *The Literary Legacy of C. S. Lewis* (New York: Harcourt Brace Jovanovich, 1979).

François Wendel, *Calvin: The Origins and Development of His Religious Thought* (New York: Harper & Row, 1960).

Keith E. Yandell, *Christianity and Philosophy* (Grand Rapids, Mich.: Eerdmans, 1984).